The Narrow Bridge

The Narrow Bridge

BY PEARL FRYE

Little, Brown and Company · Boston

1947

COPYRIGHT 1947, BY PEARL FRYE RAU

ALL RIGHTS RESERVED, INCLUDING THE RIGHT
TO REPRODUCE THIS BOOK OR PORTIONS
THEREOF IN ANY FORM

FIRST EDITION

Published October 1947

*Published simultaneously
in Canada by McClelland and Stewart Limited*

PRINTED IN THE UNITED STATES OF AMERICA

To
LOWELL SANFORD RAU

The Narrow Bridge

1

Two Hawaiian soldiers were pacing the deserted dock. Their dusky uniforms merged into the wood and brick of the pier behind them. Atop a warehouse with blacked-out windows staring blindly at the sea a white sentry swung mechanically about, the steel and stock of his rifle flashing in the downpour of tropical sunlight. Then, according to the silences and secrecies of war, the sister transports slipped their lines: first the requisitioned *Maholo,* then the larger *America,* backed into the channel. The soldiers watched the water widening between the ships; and although the passengers aboard the transports pressed the rails, tears steaming the eyes that searched the vacant shore, they did not wave. Suddenly and unwillingly the passengers murmured among themselves.

Along the swarming decks they turned to one another, smiling grimly. The security of land at last relinquished, they began to speak.

"They say the *Maholo* is shipping fifteen hundred passengers!"

"D'ya think we got fifteen hundred aboard here?"

"I heard they're below deck — the wounded from Midway. See that fellow over there? He's off the *Yorktown* . . ."

"God! Then we lost her!"

"Bottoms up! Secret to everyone but the Japs."

"They was trying for us again."

"No, they were heading for Alaska."

"They laid a smoke screen around Pearl Harbor though."

"We're casting off the tug! We're on our own!"

There was no one to sing *"Aloha Oe."*

Helen Marin leaned against the rail as intensely alert as a cat on a limb, slim and smart in her white linen suit. As her tousled hair whipped across her eyes and mouth, she constantly freed the locks with her hand, staring dry-eyed back at the green folds of Tantalus above a tawny Punchbowl. Her eyes followed the white scimitar streak of Waikiki, then lifted into the line of eternal mists lying along the green mountains.

Anxiously, Helen sought the speck — above the town, high on the heights dividing the Nuuanu and Pauoa valleys — that had been her home. Her eyes slid away from the view; she shrugged nervously. The speck was just a vacant house, the life and purpose flown out the windows, yet it was but three days since she and her thirteen-year-old stepdaughter, Jacqueline, had locked the door and gone to the Young Hotel.

"I wonder if Daddy knows we've gone?" Jacqueline said, braiding herself into the railing beside Helen, and glancing Ewa way toward the green sprawl of hills behind Pearl Harbor. "What if he's on that cruiser right now?" She pointed to a lean sharp craft lying out at sea waiting to convoy the liners home. "We'd meet him in San Francisco — "

Helen shook her head. "He's not on that cruiser."

"Do you know?" Jacqueline whispered, a little haughtily. She regarded her stepmother as something she'd had all her conscious life without having had anything to say about it.

"Perhaps he's in the South Pacific . . . perhaps he's in Alaska . . ." Helen shrugged. It was nothing these days to break up a family, crumble it like a clod and scatter it to the four winds. Angrily, Helen tossed back her curls, looking about her.

"There go the *leis* into the water — we're leaving Diamond Head!" Jacqueline squealed, clutching her mother's arm. She stripped a necklace of flowers from her shoulders and flung it farther back than any.

A man's voice asked, "Where's your *lei?*"

Helen had been brushing elbows with first one passenger and then another without regarding anyone. Now she turned to the young lieutenant speaking to her.

"Where's your *lei?*" he repeated. "I didn't see you throw one in." His was a gentle boyish face, its natural shyness overcome for the moment by the general excitement.

"It's a promise to return," Helen frowned, "and I'm not sorry to leave." He looked so frightened by her frown, she gave him a friendly smile explaining, "Life pushes me forward so fast I stub my toes if I look back."

He nodded soberly. "That's true — very true. . . . I've been assigned out here two years. I've never really disliked the Islands so much as I — I've" — he relaxed and instantly became voluble —

"been like a fish from cold water swimming around in warm tea!"

"Only it smells worse," Jacqueline volunteered, forgetting her tears as she hung momentarily limp as a ribbon over the rail, her blond hair streaming across her face.

"People are always trying to deceive you, too. . . . The same men who cried to us to help them when they were attacked."

"Unfortunately," Helen murmured, deciding that he was the right sort by the cut of his nose and chin and the quiet accent of good schools, "they didn't cry soon enough."

"That's true — very true. Have you lived here long?"

"Four years."

"They say that the time to leave, you know, is when the toy train that runs through Pearl Harbor to Haliewa begins to look like the Super Chief!" He beamed at his little joke.

Helen nodded. "That's what my husband tells me."

He frowned. "Husband in the service?"

"Yes, he's a doctor — lieutenant commander — we were civilians." And the recollection of the new status recalled also the naval traditions, the petty codes and courtesies. "It will be pleasant to see the mainland, won't it?" Helen edged away.

The lieutenant scowled sadly and nodded. "Yes. . . . I'm shipping home for keeps . . ." And as he turned to stare at the *leis* floating like betrothal rings on the waves, Helen saw for the first time the scarlet dent in his temple.

There would seem to be nothing in the course of normal existence that could knot together the three women who sat sunning themselves in the center of the ship's deck. They were as haphazardly chosen as survivors cast up on a life raft. Helen Marin sat between the haggard girl holding her baby and the woman sleeping with her mouth open. Jacqueline circled them, swinging by one arm past the roaring ventilators in an endless track over the ropes and kegs, and back around the ventilators. She was humming to herself.

"Sit down, Jackie!" Helen leaned forward catching her arm. The girl crouched sulkily. Helen continued to sit forward, a nervous instrument strung up into the wind; her green eyes searched the horizon. A delicate thrust of neck balanced a neat round head circled in dark ringlets. Jacqueline knew her stepmother was prettier than either of the other women, but the knowledge aroused only fleeting pride. She had never loved Helen as a real mother, although her father had married Helen when Jacqueline was less than a year old. Neither her father nor Helen ever mentioned Jacqueline's own flesh mother, who had died when she was born.

"May I hold the baby, Mrs. Marshall?" Jacqueline asked suddenly. She avoided her stepmother's frown like a puppy cringing stubbornly over a shoe. If Jacqueline had a baby she would rock it and protect it and never let it cry. She would hold it always, tight against her — at least, so she imagined.

"No, Sue, she musn't. Don't pay any attention to her!" Helen shook her head at the pastel-tinted girl hugging the tiny infant swaddled in blankets and sweaters.

"I don't mind, Helen, if she wants . . . if you don't mind . . ."

Jacqueline's heart leaped triumphantly. She smiled at her stepmother to catch her attention, then narrowed her eyes and stabbed her with a sneer. Helen shuddered. This was the maddening conflict she always felt when dealing with the child: sympathy that the child could not always be indulged and disgust that the child demanded indulgence or turned on her snarling.

One winter in New York, for a meteoric season, the world had hailed Helen's genius as a dancer. She had married James in the spring. Crippled the following summer, she had despised the compensation of security her marriage offered. Nursing her restlessness and boredom selfishly, her perspective had been distorted. At last the force of outward circumstances, acting like a lens, had brought vision into focus.

She knew, now, and hated the unreasoning, the illogical, minds of the selfish. Instead of riding the currents, she sought always the narrow swaying bridge across the precipitous chasms, above the tumultuous cataracts of human nature.

Jacqueline rocked the baby, cooing. Saliva bubbled nauseatingly at the corners of her mouth. "Really, Helen, I don't mind when I'm right here," Sue was saying.

Helen shrugged, smiling wryly. Sue the eternal diplomat, the gentle spontaneous friend as well!

"Christ, what heat!" The third woman rose yawning from her after-lunch trance, fumbling in the pockets of her jacket for her cigarettes. Her diamond-studded hand clumsily fingered the small cylinders as she lit a match with her thumbnail. She cleared her throat. "Helen — Sue — No, no, have one of mine." She held out the crumpled pack.

The three sat smoking silently.

Jacqueline soon tired of rocking the baby, but would not stop. She sniffed the familiar odor of food and fresh paint and tar that seemed to be, with the hum of the engines, the essence of ships at sea. She felt the sticky damp of the metal on the hatch at her back, felt the eternal moisture braiding a mop of her long blond hair. Constantly now, for the last four days, the smell and hum, the sliding away of waves . . .

Sue bent down and took the baby. "Time for his bottle, Jackie!" Jacqueline pouted prettily, but she was glad to stretch and lean against her mother. She watched drowsily as Sue, frail and sad, stepped down into the cabins.

The largest woman of the three, the hacking, amply chinned one, crunched out her cigarette and stood up stretching. "Do my seven turns around the boat deck — coming?" Jacqueline caught a subtle hint of contempt leveled at her mother. Tears of pride flooded her eyes.

"Mother's so trim already, Mrs. Brassfield!"

"Jackie!"

"Hah!" Jane Brassfield stamped away. As she turned the corner into the wind her heavy bronzed face was set, her small hazel eyes beady and bitter. Her lavishly ringed paws were again fumbling in her jacket for her cigarettes. She cupped her hands against the cloying ocean breeze and dragged the damp smoke deep in her lungs. Coughing and hacking, head bent, she strode down the slanting deck, her jacket flung back, her flat shoes silent on the aged wood.

As the ship mounted the swells, she stepped hard against the rise, bracing for the sideways roll. Over and over again her thoughts were grinding grooves deeper and deeper in her brain.

Kids . . . mean cussed kids . . . And Jack — my crazy Jack . . . She fixed her gaze on the horizon, just beyond the *Maholo* and the cruiser escort, where the sky met the curved line of water. . . . Damn Helen anyway about as useful as a spayed bitch to her husband . . . And Jack is killed, and Jerry is killed. . . . Then, because one groove veered into another: Those God-damn Japs!

Jacqueline sat pouting her lips and trying to reabsorb her tears before Helen saw them.

"Jackie, why did you have to say such a thing to Mrs. Brassfield?"

Jacqueline knew she was wicked, but she could only shake her head. She would die a thousand tortures now rather than say the words: Because you are crippled. She kicked at the water kegs lashed to the deck.

"Well?"

"Aw . . . she's an old bat!" And she thumped the casks with her toe.

Helen frowned at her knitting. "She's bitter because of her son, Jackie." She purled twice, knit twice, then dropped her knitting in her lap. "The way you and I think of Kim."

Instantly the name brought them close, remembering.

≈≈≈≈

"Kim! Kim, you rascal boy!" Ahulani Ferrara, Helen Marin's cook, had placed her hands on her broad hips and, leaning back, peered up the slim curving trunk of a coconut palm. There was a warning crack and a coconut thumped at her feet. "You rascal boy! You want kill Ahulani!"

Kim, his bare feet clinging to the rough bark, his knees clasping the trunk, turned and laughed down at his foster mother. Her fine brown face was grinning up at him, and her huge frame, planted squarely in front of a delicate fern palm, was like part of the mother earth. A soft breeze caught her hair and blew it across her eyes, ruffling the tissuelike petals of the pale hibiscus stuck over her left ear.

Kim's black eyes snapped. "Hi, Kamehameha!" he shouted to a dusky toddler hugging his mother's thigh, but one of her huge litter. "Look out below!" And down crashed another coconut. Ahulani squealed and shook with laughter like a gorgeous chocolate custard in her loose Mother Hubbard. Before she could scold him, Kim had scrambled backward down the tree and was gathering the nuts in his arms. Beside brown Ahulani and Kamehameha, Kim's skin was yellow ivory, his body fragile, and his laughing eyes small, snapping, Japanese.

Kim was Ahulani's boy in spirit and by papers only. Ahulani had found the tiny squalling infant by the stream where she went to gather water cress. Sometimes Ahulani wondered what nameless father and mother peered out of Kim's face into hers, for his was delicate, his thin nose aristocratically arched. The only clue the police had found, soon after the papers made public that an infant had been abandoned in the upper valley, was that an unidentified Japanese girl, but recently a mother, had drowned herself in the stream.

Kim gathered three huge coconuts the size of footballs and held them up for Ahulani to test. The children paused excitedly to listen for the gurgle of the milk. Then with Kim leading the way they tumbled over the ground, rolling and shouting. Kim gathered bougainvillea and stuck it in his hair, his ivory face peered like a heathen spirit of good cheer from under the magenta blossoms.

"The best nuts for Mrs. Marin, Kim!" Ahulani commanded him, and raising her skirts waddled merrily up the walk to the white house with the high pitched roof and wide low eaves. "Yoo-hoo!" she shouted. "You asleep yet, Mrs. Marin?"

Helen got up from her couch on the *lanai*. Shooing the mosquitoes that hung about the screen door like hungry cats, she opened it for Kim and his armload of nuts.

"How are the mangoes?" she asked as the nuts thudded softly in the kitchen sink . . . one – two – three – four . . .

Then the thud became the thud of depth-charges and bombs. Helen jerked awake and looked around, weak and listless, saturated with sunlight. The glint of waves bit her eyes. Her pulse beat in her ears as dark shapeless forms swam in front of her. She glanced down at Jacqueline who sat absent-mindedly gnawing at the knee clasped in her arms. Her left foot was kicking at the neat little pyramid of kegs lashed to the ship deck. Drowsily Helen watched the toe striking the kegs.

"Must you do that, Jackie?" She tapped the swinging leg. Jacqueline stopped obediently.

≈≈≈

"Too soon mangoes. Later. Bye and bye," Ahulani had explained.

"Long time after Christmas, Mrs. Marin," Kim assured her. "But papaya good for all time."

James, lean and tall in white slacks and polo shirt, strode in from the living room. "What's this, Kim, you expect doctor to crack nuts? You lazy boy, go on now, I'll give each of you a nickel if you'll peel the fiber off for me!" He had waved the cluster of youngsters out of his house. With Kim bossing the procedure, ten little pairs of feet and hands set to work on the nuts peeling off the fibrous outer coat in no time.

"Look here!" James caught Ahulani by the arm and pointed to the calendar on the wall. "I should have paid you yesterday, Saturday, and you didn't say a word. I don't always remember. . . . I'll bet they missed you and your tribe at the Five and Ten last night!"

"What day is today?" Helen interrupted him.

"The thirtieth of November." James reached over her shoulder and fixed the date with his forefinger.

"Oh, James, it can't be! The last mail ship before Christmas sails Friday . . . the *Maholo* — December fifth."

"And did you do your Christmas shopping early, Helen darling?" James turned her around, shaking his head at her.

Helen lowered her eyes dismayed. "But I had no idea it could be the thirtieth! Really, I was going to . . . by doing a little at a time I wouldn't get so tired . . ." She let her eyes plead for her.

But James looked past her as he said gently, "O.K., idiot. We'll shop together at night — and as usual — I'll enjoy the crowds after I've slaved all day!"

"James, I'm sorry. . . . You know I don't *want* to be a burden, don't you?" She laughed a gay little laugh, but kept her eyes serious.

"Sure. Sure. You're just an idiot and you do it every year!"

Helen wasn't listening. "Mail packages the fifth . . . our party the sixth . . . You know, Ahulani, I still can't decide what hors d'oeuvres . . ."

≈≈≈

Helen stirred uneasily. Shading her eyes from the sun she glanced again at the ocean. It sparkled and danced in the patches of streaming sunlight, heaving like a black satin breast in the shadows. Waves like jagged chunks of obsidian glistened under low clouds. Three glossy porpoises arched out of the water, breaking the illusion of an imperforate surface, reminding Helen of the cold black world beneath her.

There was impartial reality: The bottom of the ocean, rippled, dark, teeming with branches of bizarre shapes, slithering with unreasoning monsters. There was not even a gull to answer her if she screamed when she drowned, only the gurgling settling of the ship deeper and deeper into the mud.

Helen brushed her hand across her eyes. This was not fear, she told herself, but an appreciation of what lay ahead, an awareness that she hadn't felt before the war came thundering about her. Recognition of fact: the armor of her sanity.

There were three thousand ordinary human beings in the convoy — and yet no sign, no whisper of panic. Some seemed a little nervous and, of course, that Mrs. Sparrow was frankly scared to death! How they walked, the children and the mother! Hanging on, not looking over the rail nor drinking in the sea air, but unhappy and distrustful as cats on a raft! Helen suddenly chuckled out loud, burying her face in her hands and smiling into the dark cup of her fingers. No, she wasn't afraid, not any more.

Once James had marveled how she, in spite of her game leg, had clambered high on a pinnacle of rock. He'd called it bravery, possibly bravado. This was neither. James had even bragged to their friends about her climb, and yet he had never marveled when she kept calm, alone with Jacqueline, during the air raid. However, the climb had been before the war, when heroics and Spam were still new on the market.

As she sat staring across the water, where at any

moment a periscope might appear, she recalled how quickly she had spent her bravado, allowing herself to indulge in backseat driving all the way home from Kahuku to Honolulu.

≈≈≈

On the windward side of the island the road edged the water, sometimes turning inland over sodden rice fields or through acres of sugar cane; never, however, venturing far from the ocean into the silent canyons between the sharp volcano hills. A miserable road, it was hardly adequate to support the sudden influx of workers from the mainland who had come to fortify Oahu, the Gibraltar of the Pacific.

James had watched Helen peeling the little apple banana he'd purchased as a prize for fearlessness. He knew by the way she bent intently over the fruit she thought he was driving too fast. Helen was full of ridiculous whims that were not to be reasoned away. Hadn't it been Helen and not James who had met the locomotive in the middle of the night? Funny, he hadn't been hurt. Now, here he was driving within the law — perhaps ten miles over the island limits. He jerked the wheel sharply to the left, honked, jammed on the brakes at exactly the right moment, and easily avoided a group of youngsters wandering four abreast down the road. Their careless narrow shoulders shrugged defiance. One leaped in the air and whistled as the car streaked by. James's nostrils flared.

"Damn imps! Always in the way. They know a car can't be expected to slow down for them!" He frowned at their brown-skinned faces grinning in the rear view mirror, receding backward toward the vanishing point in the road. "Just daring me, weren't they!" He glanced at Helen, who was listening with sarcastic attentiveness while little expressions of boredom and rebellion tried to push through her mask.

Helen let the argument die for lack of interest, and looked coolly back at the fleeing landscape. This was rural Hawaii with its stiff papaya trees, saucy mynah birds and wind-frayed banana plants. There, close to a tiny corrugated iron home, was a banyan tree, its heavy horizontal branches extending long feelers at right angles back down into the earth, where they grew new roots. A group of children, all ages and sizes and in astonishing variety as well as gradation of races, was using the tree and its hundred trunks most happily for hide-and-seek.

"I'd have a swing from every limb," Jacqueline was saying. "You might be able to get us up to sixty along here, Daddy. Please go fast!" She was hanging between Helen and James, balanced on the back seat, her right elbow pressing into the back of Helen's neck.

Helen eyed her stepdaughter angrily. Jacqueline, too! They both forgot the driving hurt her. They always forgot. Jacqueline was just like her father. There was no trace of Mathilde, the little blond nurse he had married when he was an interne, and abandoned when, as a doctor, he had met Helen. Charming and aloof, surrounded by admirers, her apparent inaccessibility had challenged him. Should she have married him when Mathilde died? But Helen, the dancer, had never questioned the future.

Just then the car bounced over a bridge, and an Oriental soldier, obviously of Japanese descent but dressed in the United States Army uniform, eyed them politely, nodded and continued his march up and down.

"They never used to guard bridges," Helen had murmured, her anger burning low. "I suppose it's part of the fortification."

"Sure. Gives the soldiers something to do. . . . I'd like to get over the Pali before dark," James muttered to his wrist watch. "I've a call to make. Mrs. Wynfield's heart — suffers a lot, poor old soul."

"And so do I," Helen whispered jealously. James apparently did not hear.

The road swung to the right and they headed for the hills to leave the windward side. A precipitous mountain range leaned, buttressed, niched and covered with moss, into the wind. Honolulu lay across the pass on the lee side of the island.

For nearly a thousand feet, the rocks rose unscalable. A tortuous road crawling with impatient traffic inched its way along the face of the mountain until it reached the crest of the Pali where two currents of air roughed the cars and whistled over the precipice.

Helen looked back on the road they had come. The drop was sheer, and here in history a thousand warriors had fallen to their death. Helen closed her eyes. On this spot King Kamehameha drove the enemy headlong down like grains of dirt falling from a stone wall. Helen, listening to the shrieking of the wind, thought she heard the thousand screams falling away out of hearing. . . . In spite of the heat, her hands were clammy.

Beyond, edging the island, the snarling froth of the coral reef guarded the shore line; below, and to the left, the staccato line of trees on a ridge, the pale turquoise of a lagoon; and a lone airplane coming to rest at Kaneohe ruffled the water in a narrow wake. Across one side of the sky a rainstorm dropped a hazy curtain, and at their backs the sun beat down unmercifully.

Reluctantly, James turned the car down into the damp heat of the Nuuanu valley, winding past thready waterfalls, through jungles of vines and ferns and gnarled exotic trees, down across the stream, down to the houses, the beginning of the bus line, down past the late Queen's summer cottage, past the rambling spacious cemetery where rich *haole kamaaina* families planned to lie down and sleep someday — where three thousand people would be buried in one week, next week — down past the first gasoline station, the first drive-in stand, down, down into Honolulu where the heat lay like a soggy woolen blanket across the backs of the people.

The everlasing heat of the tropical sun . . .

≈≈≈

Thank God she'd left that forever. Helen picked up her knitting and clicked away to a deliberate rhythm playing counterpoint to the rise and fall of the ship.

2

"May I share this hatch with you?" the young lieutenant with the scarlet dent in his temple was smiling shyly, tugging at his trousers to ease the knees, his thin body bent awkwardly. He stayed that way until Helen nodded.

"Please do." She made a space for him. He sat. He coughed and looked about him. Discovering he had upset her knitting bag, he leaped up, murmured "Excuse me," blushed and sat down again. Helen continued knitting. With eager solicitude he studied every stitch she made, comforted by her apparent calm after his recent giddy, but exhilarating, climb over his own reticence.

Helen appraised the round bony head, large attentive ears and smallish delicate features, as belonging to some highly specialized breed of man.

She rather dreaded and fully expected him to break out in an analysis of abstract space. He was tall, slim, possibly enervated. As Helen's needle went in and the yarn over she felt his glance lift momentarily in spontaneous compliments, then drop again watching anxiously for the next stitch, hopeful perhaps that sooner or later she'd drop a stitch and he could tell her so. Helen wondered, should she drop a stitch?

"Is that — " he began.

"Are you by — " their voices rang together. They laughed.

"Is that your little girl by the railing?" he cleared his throat and blinked. There was nothing easy about him, yet it was this very awkwardness that aroused Helen's sympathy.

"Jackie? Yes — or rather, no — my husband's." She caught a flicker of his eyebrow. She froze. Here it comes, she told herself, and bent her head to hide her pain. But as he seemed unable to express the thought that moved the eyebrow, Helen turned from the defensive. "My name is Helen Lovejoy Marin." He grasped her hand gratefully, and produced a blush.

"I'm Jeffry Chase."

"And you're from Maine," Helen interrupted. He

nodded simply, innocently pleased to be so accurately classified, while concentrating hard on his next speech.

"And you are the dancer . . . I've seen your picture but I never saw —" politely bridging all mention of her past with an honest, "You never danced in Maine, you know."

"I don't dance any more," Helen groped nervously in her knitting bag for her cigarettes. He watched helplessly, lacking either cigarettes or matches.

"Families are better than careers, aren't they?" He broke off blushing, and his hand automatically touched his scar as he smiled gamely.

His smile soothed Helen's sensitivity. "Jeff, you're a dear." The gentle intensity of her voice made him shrink inside.

He looked at her in terror. "What?"

Helen's fingers squeezed his arm. She frowned anxiously as her green eyes searched his. "I'm sorry you're hurt, Jeff — terribly sorry."

"How did you know?" his hands were trembling on his knees.

Helen smiled wryly. "You know I didn't give up my career, Jeff. I drove my car in front of a train." She kissed him and stood up. He leaped up, too, kicking her knitting bag across the deck. As he lurched away to rescue the yarn Helen called, "Wait for me here, what you need is a tonic. . . ."

Blushing furiously he grappled with the knitting, knotting it hopelessly and stuffing it into the bag. Helen stepped jauntily away.

As the cabin door swung behind Helen, Jacqueline sauntered back to the hatch and sat down beside Jeff.

"Hello — Jacqueline — "

"Hullo."

"Your mother said for me to wait here, Jacqueline."

"Uh huh. . . . She's not my mother, though, not really," Jackie smoothed the back of her hair.

"You must love her dearly, even so, don't you? She's very pretty."

"*Ummm*, uh huh." Jackie thrust out her lower lip. "She looks awfully old when she's not wearing lipstick."

"She is beautiful!" Jeff stated desperately, hoping to win the argument by sheer force of conviction.

Jackie squirmed. She had heard her grandmother say that James left Mathilde because of Helen's beauty. Her real mother's relatives said the premature baby hadn't caused Mathilde's death so much as her angry, desolate knowledge of drugs. Jackie remembered hearing her grandmother say in a dry and breathless voice, "God intended there should be no child born of that sinful marriage when with His own hand He stopped the warning wig-wag at the railroad crossing. . . . Fate has cast the first stone!" Grandma Kendrick mixed her metaphors at will. Jackie recalled the hush of understanding that had fallen among the women.

Jacqueline frowned at the water casks at her feet. The thought of Mathilde was dark. She rubbed her hands together shivering. The cooling sun marking the ship's progress out of the tropics caressed the back of her neck without warmth. She was like an old woman, skeptically uneasy in spite of the sun and bulky life-jacket she was compelled to wear.

Looking beyond Jeff she saw a navy enlisted man entangled in wires and earphones and mouthpiece. He wore a kapok jacket belted with an automatic. Jacqueline felt sorry for him, living in danger to guard the lives of others. She hated the physical exertion of danger.

Her eyes traveled down the slim figure to the

point where the tightness of the trousers across the hips secretly arrested her. The man reminded her of Kim, although he was much older. Kim, too, had lean swaggering hips. His jeans were always about to slip off, and he never stood still or silent for an instant. He hadn't been like the boys at the private school, who were so well-mannered they were just like the girls. Jacqueline had never told her schoolmates about Kim, she would have been ashamed to, for although the color line was not her barrier, the servant was.

≈≈≈

Morning after morning they had wandered up the misty enchanted valleys of Oahu. Together they had crossed into magic places of hidden waterfalls and lush hills, wandered under scarlet poincianas and gnarled monkey-pods. As the years had passed, their friendship became a hard bond urging them in their unconscious efforts to grow up. Their play became the wild clawing battles of adolescent animals. For Jackie this love was already tortured by implacable social *Kapu*, and in the futile bitterness of recognizing his place, Kim fought to maintain his boyish superiority. The morning Jackie recalled most vividly he had just vanquished her at throwing things, hitting square at fifty paces the tomcat rear of her mother's cat, Black Pete. Jacqueline had scolded Kim for cruelty and flounced in the house. When she had looked out again Kim was playing with the Ferrara children and acting unnecessarily gay.

None the worse for wear was Pete, purring to himself on the warm vibrating lid of the washing machine. He had drunk his fill of soapy water from the laundry trays, and curled up in the sun. Idly he watched the neighbor's striped cat sneak through the lattice, peer out from under the harsh pink blossoms of the firecracker vine, then tiptoe to his saucer of milk. Finishing it, she sat down with a plaintive mew for more. The tomcat cocked his ears at her, narrowing his eyes, provoked by her display of poor breeding (she was a canefield *popoki*, an untutored cat). Pete's eyes considered the possibilities of killing a pale dove. He licked his paw once, twice, yawned and dozed.

"Scat!"

Black Peter leaped, diving into the atmosphere, his forepaws outstretched, then lifting his slim body up into the air again by the imperceptible beat of his hind feet striking the pavement. He sat on a lattice above Ahulani's head and sneered at her.

"Yoo hoo! Ahulani, is Mrs. Marin home?" a sleek Chinese woman called from the path that wound among the houses on the hill. Pete turned and fixed her with his sober eyes.

"Mrs. Marin gone downtown, Miss Ling," Ahulani grinned, wiping her soapy hands on her apron and opening the washing machine. "She be back any minute. Will you wait? . . . Have an orange," she proffered magnanimously, slapping the twenty baby hands that plunged like fruit flies into the basket on the window ledge. She herded the children under the trees to play by themselves.

Polly Ling turned from the path. Slim in the sheath of her Chinese dress, she stood with her weight on her right foot, her left foot thrust deep into her sandal, the slit in her skirt revealing a bare neat leg. Thoughtfully she lit a cigarette, her large dark eyes following the suds that swirled through Ahulani's fingers.

Ahulani squeezed a lump of clothing and thrust it into the wringer. "Mrs. Marin funny. Sit most of time. Listen to music — big music — and drum on table like this," Ahulani drummed her strong brown fingers on the wringer.

"She was a dancer," Polly reminded gently, watching the smoke from her cigarette float up into a brilliant blue morning sky dabbed clean with puffs of white trade clouds. She made a sudden rippling dance gesture with her lithe young body. Ahulani shook her head.

"No dance now. No dance Hawaiian style, no dance any style — no move no more much. Sit, listen, sometimes cry a little, I think, no?" Polly merely smiled and opened the *lanai* door, intending to wait inside, but the thought of dancing was infectious and as Ahulani swayed her massive hips, shuffling her bare feet upon the pavement, Polly stayed to watch. Ahulani's soapy hands began gesturing a love story, her face curled in a bright smile.

Kim, leaving the other children at their games, sprang forward laughing, and snatching a stick beat out the rhythm on a fallen coconut.

It was then that Jacqueline cried out, jealous of laughter that she did not share, and not seeing Polly in the shadow of the lattice, "Mother wants the washing on the line by noon, Ahulani!"

"Sure," Ahulani smiled; slowly the ripples in her body ceased as she took up another load of clothing. "Your mother, she want lunch on time, too, no?

Ahulani do washing all time, morning go away fast, no time get cress upstream for salad. . . . Kim! *Kim!* You rascal boy, you go fetch Ahulani cress from stream, maybe basket guavas, too. Hurry! Quick! Ahulani have too much work all time."

"What'll you gimme?" Kim grinned.

"Gimme! Gimme! You go now! What I give you? I give you good spank if you no go! Get! Scat! You rascal boy!" And Ahulani burst out laughing and slapped her knee.

Jacqueline lingered pouting, balancing on one foot. She loved to wander upstream with Kim after the cress that grew abundantly near the waterfall. And the luscious guavas!

"Kim's so slow, Ahulani! I'll make him hurry!" and she darted out of the kitchen. A coarse straw hat with a *lei* of feathers binding the crown rode the back of her head, the contrasting textures of dull straw and gleaming hair enchanting. As Kim threw her a welcoming glance his eye caressed her golden hair, Jackie forgot her pique and smiled.

Ahulani grinned good-naturedly, watching Kim trudging ahead Oriental-fashion.

"Kim grow up, proud he going to be a man

soon," she said, recalling the hint of warning her husband, Joe, had given her last night. Kim was growing fast, too fast to play with *haole* girls. Oriental girls understood those things, so did Hawaiian and even *haole* Portuguese, but not pale-haired, rich *haoles* like Jacqueline.

Joe Ferrara was Portuguese. He worked at the Red Hill storage project, underground every day. He was big and healthy. Didn't Ahulani have ten children born in these fifteen years? The doctor said this spring Ahulani must not come to hospital big with baby. It was hard on Joe.

Polly Ling suddenly crushed out her cigarette. "Tell Mrs. Marin I was here . . . or, no, never mind." She was hurt that Jacqueline had chosen not to see her.

Ahulani shrugged, she sensed the hurt and spoke of it. "The fashionable ladies and gentlemen school in Manoa where Jacqueline go — she learn bad manner there."

"You mean she's a little island princess?" Polly smiled. She turned to go; her friendship for Helen made her cautious of gossip.

Ahulani nodded. "Jacqueline, she wear sweater on wrong-way buttoned-up, and she get so hot her face red as beet and sweaty. . . . Mrs. Marin says it's foolish, but Jacqueline, she say all mainland girls wear sweater goofy!"

"Oh, of course, the mainland!" Polly paused in spite of herself. She hated mainlanders.

"Mrs. Marin not that way, she act like dam-please."

"She's different . . . she's been hurt — deep. You know, Ahulani?" They shared a knowledge of hurt with Helen that suddenly linked them.

"She tell Jackie she second-rate sub-debby in sweater in heat, and she say it's cheap-as-hell!"

Polly laughed out loud. "Why aren't there more like Helen Marin? Would you go to the mainland, Ahulani? Over there they are all like Jacqueline. They burn Negroes with gasoline and they make Orientals live like animals in tenements. Then they fight with other white nationalities for the title of super-race!"

Ahulani shrugged. Grinning slowly, wiping her hands dry on her skirt, she said: "Maybe Ahulani wash clothes long time, hands turn white. Go to California and act like big *haole* dame, no?" She doubled forward with laughter.

Kim thought that Jacqueline had everything in the world to make her happy. *Haoles* owned the ground they walked on. Everywhere they set up signs: KAPU — enclosing watersheds, whole mountains, for their pleasure. The land was not for the poor, and they must keep to the public paths. Jacqueline had pretty dresses. Jacqueline had money to spend sometimes.

"Polly Ling and Dr. Wong love. They will marry soon and sleep in the same bed," Kim said softly, at first only conscious of his class and hers, then suddenly of his color and his origin. "Sometimes men and women love and have babies even if they don't get married . . . they love so much . . ."

"I'll never sleep with a man," Jacqueline scoffed, looking quickly away.

"But, Jackie, all grownups do!"

"That's silly. . . . They do not! If they don't want to." She guessed she knew as much about it as he did.

"Oh?" Kim felt a tightening within him as he stared at her round firm body, still almost boyish. Suddenly he laughed. "It's like people kissing in pictures, uh? Makes you want to holler and whistle!"

Jacqueline deigned at last to look at him and gave him a grateful smile. She didn't feel inclined to whistle any more than Kim did, really. They both wanted something else. "Uh huh." All the same she agreed with him. "Silly lotta mush — love." And thus hiding her desire from him, she thrust her hand in his and held his long thin fingers tight.

A scarlet cardinal flashed up from the fronded maze of a fern palm, breaking aslant the streaks of light. The sun — the shade — the primal red — and then again the sun. The pure strong notes of his song were intricately throated.

Kim leaped in the air, then flung himself against a bank — embracing the earth as if, somehow, he were a basin in which God might pour the universe, the sapphire sky, the trade winds, snatches of the cardinal's song, and Jacqueline's golden hair. His knees trembled as he stood up and his heart beat painfully.

The earth was his mother and his father. Kim never bothered to believe that other lands lay beyond the curve of encircling waters. Oahu was all the earth, a mothering earth, warm and fruitful. Every day as Kim swam, or ran barefooted through the streets sniffing the heavy rich smell of wharves and ships, or flung himself upon the moss, or slept hour after hour on hard sands under a blazing sun, he knew that year in and year out it would be the same. Nature welcomed life and nourished it tenderly. Now for an instant he saw Jacqueline as part of his life. Where he had lavished his affection on all living things, he now hoarded it for her. She who was pale and pure, had she, too, felt the change?

They had climbed to the head of the stream where the waterfall fed it. A perpendicular rock leaned out, pouring a delicate mist down into a pool clogged with purple water lilies and water cress. The rock seemed to make a natural diving place for the children who came to swim, — but all shunned it, for underneath the surface of the water, hidden by the lilies, lay ragged lava rocks.

Kim whispered suddenly, "Gee, Jackie, you look swell in pink . . . you're beautiful!"

"Oh?" Jacqueline smiled wisely even as she let her fingers stay in his.

"We'll marry someday — won't we?" With fingers trembling shyly Kim stroked her hair. Jacqueline pressed against him.

He bent down and kissed her, lightly, on the head. Jacqueline giggled. Suddenly she clutched at his shirt, tearing the buttonholes with her hot fingers.

"Kim! We'll swim. Take off your clothes. . . . I

want to see how you look naked, Kim, if I'm to marry you!" With shrilling laughter she screamed, "Are you yellow underneath your clothes — all the way? Little and thin and yellow?"

Kim gasped, startled, hurt. Then his black eyes narrowed as he shrank back. Abruptly he clutched at the cress in the water, jerking it up in long wet strands. Jacqueline stared with dying amusement, slowly sensing something had smashed.

≈≈≈

Jacqueline's back stiffened and she kicked again at the water kegs. The memory was cruel. Shivering, she glanced at the young officer beside her who lay like a stone image staring back, squinting along the streak of wake. Only when Helen reappeared on deck did he sit up, a quiet intensity in his appraising eye. Jackie buried her face in her hands as Helen came with a rhythmic step craftily plotted to hide any trace of limping.

She sat down without a word, setting before her a bottle of Scotch and two small empty creamcheese glasses.

"Just the medicine you need," she told Jeff. ". . . We both need," she added. "My therapy is drastic, and very obviously temporal. . . . Ooh

. . ." She threw her knitting bag over the Scotch and glasses just as the Chaplain hove in sight.

Jeff leaped up guiltily and put two or three decorous feet of deck between Helen and himself. He then assumed a theatrically angelic expression of such innocence Helen knew he had imagined rape.

The Chaplain exchanged salutes with Jeff and that was all. Jeff heaved a sigh and sidled back to Helen.

"Hypocrite," she beamed.

He blushed and sat down unable to think of an excuse, letting the hypocrisy of her hidden Scotch go unscored.

"Mum's the word, Jackie, old girl." Jeff indicated the Scotch. Jacqueline smiled contemptuously and stood up.

"Good-by, Mumsie." She cocked her head at Jeff. "One coke every morning until we dock, served here on the hatch, sir — or I'll tell!"

"Jackie!" Helen had to protest because the horror on Jeff's face demanded it.

"Oh, yes I will!" Jackie pranced about them. "I'll tell! I'll tell!" she winked at Jeff, shaking her head at him. "I'll tell . . ." And off she skipped.

"Will she?" Jeff gasped.

"Will she what?" Helen handed him a scant half-inch of fluid in the bottom of a cheese glass.

"Tell on me?" Jeff took the glass, eyed it uneasily, then gulped it down. Smothering a strangling cough he tucked the glass behind her knitting bag.

"What is there to tell on you?" Helen shrugged.

Jeff twisted his neck in his collar. "I guess," he said finally, "there's nothing to tell . . . is there?"

He began to unravel the snarls he had made in Helen's yarn. As the thread came free Helen took it and wound it into a neat round ball. There were intricate knots to be solved, complicated by meaningless twists and loops. The obvious solution usually led only to worse tangles.

"As I grew up," Jeff began to speak confidently at last, "I was told that the purpose of life was to make man strive to be ideal. The means to which had been revealed to, and practised by, my enlightened parents. It sounded fine. Yet the grass around our house was cut short, artificially fertilized, and while it grew quite green it had to be re-seeded often. . . . Anyway, I went dutifully to school and studied hard, because I was promised that diligence would be rewarded. In the meantime my family encouraged the girl they believed

— and rightly — I was too serious about to marry my chum. Naturally, they knew best — considered in the light of my future (the future *they* planned) didn't they? Black — white. I stuck to the righteous white, like a kid hopping the cracks in the pavement. . . . I battled valiantly and overcame all physical instincts that were not according to the ideal." He stopped, working intently at a knot; slowly it came away except for one provocative loop that stayed where it pleased. Helen produced a hairpin. The yarn loosened, she wound it slowly.

"You were all right, Jeff, trying to stick to the black and white. . . . But you had a right to explore for yourself," she murmured.

"Do you really think that?" For a moment his eyes were brightly bold. "I did want to explore . . ."

"And did you ever?"

"No."

Wandering back, Jacqueline saw Helen's knitting needles slacken. Jeff had gone. The glasses were empty and drying in the sun.

3

ON THE FIFTH DAY OUT OF HONOLULU THE WORLD shrank to the width of the deck. Bellowing leviathan moans, the ship edged cautiously. Thirty thousand tons stopped dead by the flowing airy nothingness of fog. . . . There! Listening ears were pricked by the bos'un's whistle and the ship's horn. The sister ships were calling back and forth, locating one another.

Helen limped along the deck, cautiously feeling her way in the mist, searching for Jacqueline. She quickened her step somewhat as she walked, for none of the passengers who might have noticed her seemed eager to brave the dreary damp cold on deck.

Helen paused, having found Jacqueline leaning against the rail. She looked about her. The world had turned gray, neutral, aloof. Only the sleek antiaircraft guns, their metal greased, their pink-skinned attendants polishing them, shone out of the fog. Helen's mind hesitated, hovering over a multitude of images.

≈≈≈≈

There had been a wild and lovely garden on Oahu. Then the soldiers came and planted a gun.

James had stood back to admire it respectfully, as men will a machine, while she had felt sudden anger boiling within her.

"It's loathsome . . . loathsome . . ." she had sobbed suddenly, right there in front of the soldiers, making James turn on her in disgust.

"What the hell's the matter with you?"

She was running into the house, around and around through the rooms, clenching her fists, until, finally exhausted, she had dropped on the bed. She lay there biting her handkerchief to shreds, driving her fist into the pillow.

"Nerves . . . War and all," James had explained to the soldiers. She sobbed more wildly still when, on coming in the house, he chose to ignore her.

≈≈≈≈

Standing in the fog, Helen suddenly smiled to herself. Only Black Pete had mocked the gun.

≈≈≈

Helen had slept after her tantrum, but waking toward morning stirred restlessly beside James, her body hot and stiff, wrapped like a mummy in the sheet. James muttered, "Now what's the matter?" and went on sleeping.

She sat up and stared out the window. The moon glittered on the rain-soaked banana leaves and lit up a moth, big as a bird, fluttering in the dark. The silvered moss was striped with the black velvet shadows of coconut palms. Overhead puffy clouds swam lazily above volcanic hills.

Helen brushed back her damp curls and threw off the sheet. Her feet found her straw slippers on the floor. As she went to the *lanai* there was a rustling in the garden, leaves thrust aside and grasses parted; then a quick beat of paws and long claws scratching the screen betrayed Black Peter, alert as a small panther. He rolled purring on the moss, inviting her to join him. Helen stepped out into her skillfully disordered garden. The night was nearly as light as day, but silvered instead of gilt, like a song of subtle quarter-tones. . . .

The four-inch antiaircraft gun stood in the center of the garden, sleek and glistening, its nose pointed skyward, sprung back on its haunches. A searchlight flashed on across the valley, poking an inquisitive finger about in the darkness, then vanished. Helen approached the gun warily, but the cat leaped on it and, lashing his tail, balanced his way up the long shining barrel. He stuck a curious paw down the yawning snout. Helen, caught in a macabre dream, waited for the gun to roar and spit Black Peter at the moon. . . . Instead, he swung under the barrel, wrestling with it. Then without warning he dropped, dancing heedlessly away.

≈≈≈≈≈

Turning her back on the ship's guns, Helen followed Jacqueline along the deck. The wind was cold against her face; she tipped her head back that it might cool her throat. She knew too well the purpose of the gun on the ship . . . and the gun in the garden, and the ominous presence of the soldiers in their tents who had mounted guard there following December 7. . . .

≈≈≈≈≈

She had been ill while others buried the dead and ministered to the wounded. Everyone else had been busy. Jane Brassfield had been hostess to a dozen army wives, *evacuées* from Wahiawa near Schofield. James had brought daily reports of Kim; said he was coming along splendidly. Helen asked if he suffered any shock. James laughed; he apparently noticed none.

She had no sooner recovered than Jacqueline fell ill. . . .

All had been well until that evil day they had gone with Polly Ling to receive their gas masks at the neighborhood public school. Helen had shuddered when she saw the sign NO GAS MASKS FOR CHILDREN UNDER THREE, and heard the attendants say apologetically, Later perhaps . . . They are on order.

Behind the school, slums lay along Pauoa Road below the heights and up the valley bottom where poor laborers of all races, white, brown or yellow, had their tiny huts. It had been a hotter day than usual, and although the winter as a whole had been quite comfortable, that day had been unbearably hot, windy and dusty.

Jacqueline gasped, dismayed. "We're just about the only *haoles* here, Mother!"

"The soldier on duty is *haole*, Jackie, and red and hot as a *malihini!*" Polly had bent forward whispering, "And those Portuguese laborers are white . . ."

"White trash," Jacqueline sneered.

"Jackie!" Helen whispered sharply. "That's a terrible thing to say!"

Polly's eyes flashed like lightning across Jacqueline's head, but she continued smiling. "It's miserably hot, isn't it? Why don't you wear your hair on top of your head like this? Look, Helen, isn't she pretty? Now a flower — " and she plucked one out of her own hair and stuck it in Jacqueline's. The girl would have jerked away but caught a glance of admiration in the eye of a young Chinese, so she tilted her head demurely and said.

"Thank you, Miss Ling, that feels so cool."

In the dusty schoolyard under the monkey-pod trees the soldier was herding the milling people. Their yellow wrinkled faces laughed and shouted. Their grubby clothes and knowing glances suddenly goaded Helen's fastidiousness beyond endurance. For a moment she sympathized with Jackie. The Japs were awful, their cockroach scurryings, their genius for worming their way into the front of any line where there was something for the asking. She did not stop to classify each person, but lumped them all under the title of "Jap." For the moment she forgot they were United States citizens until she felt a twinge of conscience. After all, what about the exploitation of the Orient? Was our policy to be that of other nations who conquered and exploited, demanded seaports and the right to rule, only to withdraw in times of trouble, to leave the people . . . ?

"Hey, you two!" Helen turned to see the soldier at her elbow forcing two mop-haired, black-eyed boys into their proper places at the end of the line. "Sorry, ma'am," the red-faced private frowned, apologizing to Polly, whom the two boys in their wild tag had jostled out of place. Polly blushed.

"Rascal boys!" she whispered to Helen, smiling. The boys wiped their noses on their arms, pushed the hair out of their eyes and shifted self-consciously from one foot to the other. Suddenly they burst out laughing, and so did Polly.

She grabbed one moppet by the hair and shook him into submission before Helen.

"This is my brother, Isaac — a rascal boy. What do you say to Mrs. Marin?" The boy mumbled an embarrassed, "How do," and Polly began to brush the dust off his clothes while he squirmed. "Where have you been to get so dirty, Isaac?"

"We went with the military to clear brush yesterday. Everyone volunteered . . ." He managed to shake himself free, "Hirohito here, and I, worked right with the big *haole* bankers. So did your boy friend, Dr. Wong . . ." He turned shyly to Helen: "And Dr. Marin — and old man Brassfield . . . Didn't we?" and he kicked his friend in the seat of the pants, darting away.

The Japanese boy beside him blushed scarlet, and plunged like a maddened horse after Isaac. "My name is Ito. . . . I'm American!"

Polly shook her head. "They're good boys — rascal boys. The Japanese has a Russian mother. . . . Only, his uncle had to be put in a camp, he's black in his heart, that old man!"

Helen watched the boys tumbling and scuffling about the dusty yard. Suddenly she was certain God had not tinted men's skins to measure the degrees of His love. . . . Now for an instant she was reassured. She had glimpsed the narrow swaying bridge across the chasm. . . .

That was the morning — standing in line for hours listening to the gonglike voices and harsh laughter — that Jacqueline had complained of sniffles and a depressing headache.

When James came home he had made Helen leave the room and bathe with disinfectants. . . . She had smiled hysterically at Jacqueline's suffering eyes. The girl plucked idly at the blanket, and squirmed weakly when Helen stroked her forehead.

When Helen started to cry, sobbing "Jackie, darling!" James had laughed; even Jacqueline smiled. They were both alike, utterly self-sufficient.

"I'll call in Wong, Helen," James told her, looking, as he spoke, the very essence of steadiness and normalism.

"Mrs. Marin, your husband was right, of course — he did not need to call me to know that Jacqueline has typhoid," Dr. Wong patted her arm and gave her a kindly smile. "Don't worry. . . . We do everything for the little girl. You, come to my office, I give you shots — Polly better come, too. . . ." Wong's tone was exactly the tone Helen longed to hear from James. Everyone felt better after Wong had set to work.

Falling in with the others, Helen had begged to help with the nursing.

Wong only smiled, leaving James to say bluntly,

"There's nothing you could do, idiot." He shook his head, his slender nervous face solicitous only for his child, his gray eyes thoughtful. He didn't bother to look up as he said, "You'd only be in the nurse's way. Jackie's as good as gold. She'll take it in her stride."

Helen's lower lip quivered as she avoided the all-seeing eye of Dr. Wong. She knew he saw deep in her mind, and suddenly she feared what he might learn.

She no longer slept during the long hot nights Jacqueline was in the hospital, but followed Pete about the garden wishing she might sleep as heavily as James. Her lips trembled and she began to cry; weeping came easily of late, because James was imperturbable, forgetful of her. It had been weeks since he had felt even the most elementary need of her. Yet all she wanted of life was to belong, to be necessary. Long ago she had relinquished all hope of actively creating anything, either art or human being. God knew she would have gladly borne James ten children if she could. Now he ignored her very presence. He had forgotten he had told her once, "To hell with infants, dearest, so long as I have you around to decorate my bedroom!" Now she felt as meaningless as the tinsel Santa Claus hung on the artificial Christmas tree that year. James had turned him over and read aloud with ironic piety: "Made in Japan." So now, stumbling in the garden, she focused her wet eyes on Pete, gave him all her attention as his stealthy form began to climb a coconut palm.

Through her tears, Helen watched his movements up — up — the leaning trunk, until her eye froze to another eye peering out of the tree: the obscene glittering eye of a giant rat.

"Pete! Pete!" He laid back his ears, reproving her bad sportsmanship with a flick of his tail. "Peter!" Helen clapped her hands. The cat turned and darted past her into the house.

Helen fled like a ghost. She slipped into bed beside James. An arm swung lazily up and fell heavily across her breasts. "What's the matter now, idiot?"

In answer she curled against him, frightened, wanting desperately to share his sense of peace. He slept soundly, deaf and stupid to her.

The telephone rang.

Yes, Dr. Marin would come right away. . . . Of course. . . . No, not at all. . . . Did your wife obtain a night pass? Never mind, they won't stop maternity cases — yes, Dr. Marin will be there by the time you are. Is your car blacked out? . . . Not at all. . . . Good-by.

James whipped the sheet off, instantly alert. "I hope these socks match."

"Shall I black out the room?"

"No time. . . . Trousers . . . shirt . . . bag . . . Where are my shoes? Damn the blackout — I can't see. What in . . ." There was a sudden yeowl. The crash of a body against the dressing table provoked a tinkling protest from the perfume bottles. "Damn that cat! Do I have to sleep with him, too?"

"Did you hurt him?"

"Did I hurt him . . . I'll kill him!"

"Oh, no, James, no. . . . Pete! Petey, Petey Peee-ty!" And Helen clutched the cat to her as James slammed the door.

She slept uneasily. She dreamed the cat was battling a rat and that its loathsome lice were crawling everywhere, on her — on Jacqueline. And somehow, there was an aged Japanese laughing and laughing and shaking his head until it nearly rolled off his shoulders. A Chinese flower vendor trotted by carrying a bamboo pole with baskets of purple water lilies hung on either end. He shook hands solemnly with Polly who appeared encumbered with a huge gas mask. Helen was wearing a mask, too, and nearly suffocating. The roar of air through the cannister had all the horror of an anesthetizing hood. And the Japanese was laughing and shaking his head . . . *bzzz* . . . his head.

And Polly wore a halo, her dress swirled in the wind. The old Chinese trotted away, the purple water lilies bobbing, and Pete and Jacqueline came leaping toward Helen to the tune of ". . . A little brown girl in a little grass shack . . ." *bzzz* . . . water lilies cool and fresh and cats and guns and war . . .

When she woke one small mouselike thought was gnawing the shadowy dreams out of her mind. Mice — rats — cats — *cats!* That was it. She sat up straight and frail in her bed staring through the window at the vacant harbor and crinkling line of surf beyond.

The whole island lay as if under an evil spell. The docks deserted, occupied only in stealth and martial secrecy, while armed guards paced the waterfront. Occasionally a battle-gray liner lay at anchor, unidentified, its destiny unknown, then vanished in the night. Where were the gentle dazzling white pleasure ships, nosing around Diamond Head into the jubilant, singing harbor of tourist-bureau friends?

Never had the mainland seemed so far away as it did that brittle sunny morning. The clouds banked high around Mount Tantalus, the sea a cool glittering blue, the city silent between them . . .

The sharp cries of the mynah birds and the cardinals framed the fearful silences of war. Helen missed the rushing whirr of Clipper ships roaring over Honolulu, over Punchbowl, past Diamond and Koko Heads, east — toward home, east — shining silver bird-messengers worthy of Polynesian gods. . . . Instead, she heard the return of a weary dawn patrol.

The day was Jacqueline's seventeenth day of fever. Today, James might save a life or help one into it, either was all in a day's work. "It's just my job, Helen, like cooking dinner" — her stomach revolted at his simile — "feelings only interfere with good workmanship. You feel so much you weep over instead of bandaging a sore thumb!" James would pat her cheek with his slim gentle fingers. Then she remembered she was angry with him. He had said he would kill Black Pete — and he knew Pete was all she had left . . . was that why he wanted to kill him? The dirty, dirty sadist . . . Helen started to cry.

Shaking her head and rubbing her eyes, she fought back the tears. These were insane thoughts! Good God, wasn't there something she could do — besides her everlasting knitting — something to occupy her mind and her body, something that she could stand up to, something tangible? It was hell to be sick.

Opening the *lanai* door, she welcomed Pete, his tail held high like an inquisitive periscope moving among the chairs. She scooped him in her arms and whispered loving words to his flattened ears and sulking half-shut eyes. "The bad baby . . . did he steal out of his Mamma's bed to go hunting?" He flicked an ear and stole a sly glance at the cage of parakeets and sent those idiotic birds into giddy squawks and flutters.

The hammering of half-naked carpenters, their savage heads bound in bright handkerchiefs, their work punctuated by shouts of laughter and revolting hawking and spitting, rang in Helen's ears. The men were repairing the damage done December 7. The work progressed spasmodically, depending on the delayed arrivals of the necessary materials from the mainland and the whims of the crews of men.

Helen closed the hall door, but the noise continued unmuffled, for the rest of the house stood open.

Wandering into the garden, Helen felt the muscles in her shoulders draw tight, a mothlike fluttering deep inside her. The tips of her fingers were stiff and cold. The repetition of the hammers striking nails annoyed her. *Bang. Bang. Bang.* She counted: one — two — three — four. Within her brain a tiny anger began to bubble.

She caressed the cat. He was all she had to love. Black Pete, and this — she smiled to herself — this, her garden. She sank to the moss, breathing hard, her heart pounding with the hammers, her flashing eyes twin emeralds to the cat's eyes. She drove her long vermilion-lacquered nails into the clammy blue palms of her hands.

She examined her fingers. Fingers. Her cold fingers, fluttering palm-leaf fingers. The witch fingers of the croton plant sprawled in ugly twisted gestures. Blood leaves. Green and black leaves, arthritic, yellow. Unnatural is nature: gaudy and lustful. The pink buds of the creeper seeking an embrace. Strangling is the way of the vine . . . Peering out of the coconut palm, the lewd eye of the plague rat . . .

She covered her face with her hands.

The cat slept in her lap while she sat vigilant hour after hour. James had said, "I'll kill him!" And James didn't care if a gun stood in the garden, if Jacqueline died, if Kim died — and he didn't love Helen. He said, "I'll kill! Kill! Kill!" Gone was reason, vanished, everything was gone!

The day turned hot, a light rain drenched her; and the sun had warmed her again when Helen heard the car returning, crunching stealthily along the gravel, the motor switched off. . . . She smelled the intoxicating cup-of-gold, and at the corner of her eye the scarlet bougainvillea waved an angry banner. James was coming to kill Pete.

She heard the hammers again. One — two — three . . . *bang — bang — bang* . . . and James's footstep, keeping time.

Clutching the cat, Helen fled back of the house. The carpenters stopped and stared at her, an enchanting apparition in her thin silk nightgown. She looked carefully from one to the other, their faces blurred, doubled, snapped in and out of focus. Anger distorted her sight.

"Give me that!" Helen limped painfully towards a huge Hawaiian, forgetting to hide her lameness. He gawked at her. Her face was pinched and white. "Give me that!"

"The hammer?" The Hawaiian grinned. "Missus

recurring. Even now at times she felt just as faint and weak as when she had first come from the hospital.

≈≈≈≈

It was a wonder, Jacqueline had mused drowsily, twisting in bed, that the rain did not soak right through the roof. Would it never stop? It fell in a heavy sheet, drawing a gray veil along the eaves, obscuring the mountains and the grove of papaya trees that stood like feather dust mops stuck in the ground. Black Pete sat in the open window, his eyes narrowly studying a spider that walked, on legs the length of Jacqueline's fingers, across the top of the dressing table. Absorbed as he seemingly was in the spider, Pete's tail betrayed his impatience at the rain. The thin tail swished, stroke after stroke, across the ledge. Pete's back twitched with each drop of water that imprudently splashed him.

Jacqueline heard Helen, busy in the kitchen with the eternal bouillon. Mother was so tiresomely solicitous now she had Jacqueline home.

It had been a pleasant surprise to leave the typhoid hospital sooner than James had promised. He had murmured something about, "Mother needs her little girl's company," and put her to bed in her own room. He came home twice a day, to have a look. It was almost as if he felt Mother were the invalid, not Jacqueline.

Jacqueline had felt a tiny pang of jealousy. Not that she really cared — heck no — except fathers were something that belonged to you whether or not you paid any attention to them, like your umbrella or your schoolbooks. . . . She turned and stared at Pete with rising animosity.

Jacqueline had, as James said she would, taken the fever in her stride and felt no need of sympathy from Helen — or bouillon. . . . Now, however, with a returning fever, she felt painfully annoyed. Perhaps it was the soup, or the cat, or Mother. . . . Perhaps it was the color of the room.

Why had Helen chosen yellow to redecorate the bombed-out room? Yellow and ivory! Jacqueline loved pink. Nervously she pulled at the tufts on the spread. Horrid old yellow tufts! "I did want pink!" Two tears welled up in Jackie's eyes. She turned her head uncomfortably. The fever baked her.

Still it rained, and still Black Pete sat lashing his tail. After a while he rearranged his hind end on the ledge so that he stared at Jacqueline. His green eyes, exactly like Helen's, glistened in the black velvet mask of his pointed face, and the black of his fur blended into the diffused light of the rain. Jacqueline returned his stare.

After ages of plucking the spread, Jacqueline was aware only of eyes, the cat's — or Helen's — Helen's or the cat's? She wasn't sure, but she was sure of the menacing intent of the gaze. Her fingers plucked faster and faster and the yellow-ivory walls — which were not pink — reflected the silvery light. The small alarm clock on the bed table ticked frantically louder and louder.

Jacqueline heard Helen go into the living room and sit down to play the piano as she had begged before lunch. The music began gently, a sickly *valse*, a nocturne. . . . Then it snapped. The notes came tumbling and crashing out of the piano, terrifyingly loud. And although Helen sat at the piano in the living room, Jacqueline knew that by some island witchcraft Helen's eyes were glittering at her out of Pete's head. What was the wild and noisy music — *crescendo — fortissimo — crescendo* . . . ?

After that the piano leaped on Jacqueline's bed. It grinned at her and flapped its top like a menacing black wing. Each white key — white ivory to match the loathsome walls and black ivory to match Black Pete — was keeping time by beating on her head. Pete's tail lashed like a giant metronome, or was it a sharp black whip? And his eyes — or were they Helen's eyes — never blinked. . . . The alarm clock jerked its hands and slowly turned into a beating heart.

Jacqueline's fingers stretched and stretched until they were cold tentacles twining and untwining. She began to reach farther and farther . . .

The alarm clock smashed against Black Peter's neck, as Jacqueline fell back against the pillows, gasping, watching the strange spasmodic twitch in Pete's hind leg, hearing the bestial howl, seeing the final lash of his lean tail. Suddenly, she was aware the music, too, had stopped.

Helen stood in the doorway.

"He came at me," Jacqueline lied desperately, looking squarely at her stepmother, "with — with his claws!" And as she stared unblinking into Helen's eyes, she saw Pete's eyes alive again, rekindled in Helen's. She covered her face with her hands and began to moan. Slow minutes passed, ticked off by the rain dropping from the eaves.

Jacqueline kicked angrily at the rungs of the railing. Glancing up she saw her stepmother advancing through the fog. Jackie hid her face in her hands. The gesture of despair and shame had become natural.

≈≈≈≈≈

White-lipped, Helen had said, "Did he hurt you?" The tone was dry. She had scooped the dead cat into a wastebasket, shoving with a magazine to avoid touching him. Jacqueline had expected her to cry, or to be angry; at least to hug the miserable dead beast. Instead, breathing fast, her lips drawn down, Helen had left the room carrying the basket at arm's length, and never again mentioned Black Pete's name.

≈≈≈≈≈

The ships' horns called sadly, were sadly answered. The fog rolled in dense billows.

"What are you thinking about, Mumsie?" Jacqueline peered shyly into Helen's face. She saw that it was tired, the skin drawn over the delicate framework of bones. The fine lines running from the corners of the eyes broke across the blue veins of the temples. There was the brittle glaze of a terrible experience laid over Helen's young face. A look of tense ironic amusement was so fleeting when she smiled it was readily forgotten in the gay reassurance of her quick laughter. Now the smile flashed on Jacqueline.

"Thinking about?" Helen shrugged. "Oh, about Daddy, I guess."

4

THE TAN SERVICE UNIFORMS OF TWO NAVAL OFFIcers sifted from the moist curtain of fog and stopped directly in front of Helen.

"Mrs. Marin — Lieutenant George." Jeff Chase stood as if at bayonet point and stuttered through the introduction, then in excruciating embarrassment gulped a smile and withdrew. Before disappearing into the cabins he paused to look at Jackie. She returned his stare with a knowing sneer, shaking her head at him. He shuddered and vanished.

"Your husband's an old acquaintance, Mrs. Marin."

"Not really!"

"Yes, knew him years ago. Understand he's Navy, too, now. Small world, isn't it?"

Helen smiled, "Yes, very small, Lieutenant . . .

George! Of course — Connecticut — How nice to meet you! James has spoken of you so warmly — or was it your brother who was his classmate in pre-med?"

The Chaplain beamed. "My brother, yes. But I've known Jim Marin since he was knee-high to a grasshopper, so when I saw you taking such a motherly interest in that poor young Chase . . . Well, and knowing Jim, I wondered, would you help *me?*"

He paused for Helen's, "Of course," acknowledging it with a preëmptory nod, as he went on, "No desire to alarm the ladies aboard, you realize, but they musn't leave their children for a moment. . . . If you can just help me to remind them of that — I *can't* be everywhere." His voice bordered on desperation. "When you see a toddler out of bounds — "

"I'll be glad to. I really think the mothers are trying to handle the children — but some *will* escape." Helen smiled a merry friendly smile past the Chaplain's ear, as if she shared a joke with someone behind his back, perhaps with herself. He coughed uneasily.

"I've tried to arouse — " The ship's horn interrupted him. He waited patiently. ". . . To arouse interest in a party, or to organize games, but such utter apathy — such passive resistance!" He raised his eyes, and the pinched bridge of his nose seemed to brace the pained arch of the brows that reminded Helen, appropriately enough, of two little Gothic church doors.

Helen tossed back her hair impatiently. She wanted to snap, "And what of it? This isn't a Sunday excursion on the Hudson — this ship is an enemy target and we're responsible for the poor little beasts. Why shouldn't we feel apathy to potato races, and lose our tempers and slap their saucy mouths and jerk up their panties?" Instead, she said only, "Really, don't you think, Chaplain, that perhaps just a dish of ice cream and cake some noon . . . ? You see, our children haven't been drilled in war, it's just a lark to them. You can't cry, 'Hail Roosevelt! Line up for the potato race!' Not even on a navy transport."

The Chaplain laughed a rousing good-fellow laugh, and the bridge of his nose slid back down into merry lines that circled his mouth. Helen suddenly decided that she liked this gentle worrying idealist immensely. He and his four brothers must have been fun as children; no wonder James liked them still.

"Thank you, thank you, Mrs. Marin. Of course, a dish of ice cream and cake. . . . How very thoughtful. That's exactly what Jim Marin would have said: something simple and to the stomach!" He peered through the fog into her face. "It takes parents to understand these youngsters — I'd like to have a dozen of them! Ha! Ha! Hail Roosevelt!"

He rocked happily on his heels. A party at mess would be easier anyway than games all over the deck and children plopping overboard. "That will be a jolly party, won't — " He broke off, looking at Helen. A smile, a sad, bitter, angry smile, was twitching at her mouth. What was the matter with her? Good gracious, was she crying?

Helen's eyes had found the golden cross on his collar. It glowed in the fog like the powerful guns. She clapped her hand abruptly to her twitching mouth, wrestling with her will, struggling to forget and remembering more.

She saw a carved ivory fisherman in a New England parlor among Tobies, Sandwich glass and copper kettles. She heard hidden carolers singing on the eve of war, of Holy Nights, and Infants born. . . . And here the Cross on treacherous waters!

The Chaplain, overwhelmed by babies and women, stared at his feet, mumbling, pretending not to notice her distress. "All this fuss — precaution — is due to the fact we're fog bound. And at the very gates of salvation!" He made an apologetic gesture, like a gatekeeper who has lost the key. "There, listen . . . Did you hear it?"

Helen nodded, but she didn't hear it as she stared blindly at the Chaplain's cross. It made her want to weep, because by some miracle of design conceived in symbolism it was the most beautiful cross she had ever seen. She wanted to weep. Oh, fight back sentiment! She pressed her nails into her hands and threw back her head, laughing.

≈≈≈≈

"This very fine piece. No can get more. Ship no go China now." The Chinese curio dealer had turned the small ivory piece in his hand, lovingly. He peered hopefully from behind enormous horn-rimmed spectacles, wiry and sleek as a cricket. His straight silk shirt clung to his narrow shoulders, giving the lithe upper part of his body the soft grace of an undeveloped girl. "Fifty dollar. I give you ten per cent off. . . . This very fine old ivory piece . . ." He held the little figurine balanced on the palm of his hand, his fingers bent stiffly back, "Forty-five dollar!" He snatched his glasses from his nose to emphasize his offer.

The yellow light from the carved dragon teak lamps glistened on his forehead, slashed across his temple and melted into the enigmatical depth of his black eyes. The shop was stuffy with the smoke of dinner being cooked in a back room, of peanut oil and wine and garlic, and the heavy scent of the carnation *lei* that Helen wore. James loomed handsomely tall against the light, his head grazing the beams of the low ceiling. But by a trick of stagecraft, the light picked up the gleam of the energetic ivory figure; and all else, pink flesh, black teak and scarlet curtains, merged into the shadows.

"It is lovely," Helen admitted, taking it in her hand. The tiny ivory fisherman was bent by the weight of an imaginary fish caught at the end of his straining pole.

"You know good ivory. This very old. Maybe hundred year. No get more until China war is over. Come from Shanghai, but Jap block port now. You see my stock? No more can get. Get more, I sell thousand dollar easy. No get. Close shop before long, maybe!" He returned abruptly to the ivory piece. "To my very good friends, *twelve* per cent off!"

"All right," James said, ruefully unscrewing his pen, numbering and dating his stub and check with care, checking the balance brought forward.

"*Hao!*" and the dealer threw back his shoulders, doffed his spectacles as a diplomat would his hat, and clicked his heels.

Helen kept the little figure in her hand. For an instant she was melted into a tingling shimmer of happiness. So much beauty between her fingers! She opened them and peeked at it. "I like it, James," she whispered.

"It will do very well for Mother's gift."

"Yes." And Helen gripped it harder. She tried to imagine it on the shelf in his mother's colonial parlor. No matter. In this moment it was completely possessed. For this instant it had been laboriously created — for this and the handful of pennies paid the sculptor. Slowly she handed it to the curio dealer. No need to look at it now, it was implanted in her.

"There is a handsome vase," James was saying, moving toward a dream of soft brown glaze decorated with dull violet and green and ivory figures. It was magnificent, Helen knew, and worth many more dollars than James earned every month. But she had been pierced too deeply by the ivory figure to withstand another ecstasy. Better to remember limited incomes and Jacqueline's Christmas bicycle, and the new hat for Ahulani . . . "Do you like it?" James persisted.

"Yes," Helen's answer was indifferent, the strength gone out of her. Disappointment slowly blotted out the pleasure in James's eyes. Good God! Was there no understanding his wife? He reminded himself of her sickness. The pain was nearly gone, the paralysis massaged away, but somewhere there were nerves still sick. He knew the antidote was patience. Infinite patience, James, even if it drives you mad! Infinite understanding to be lavished on a whim now bound relentlessly to him by a physical love from which he could not free himself.

James knew the necessities of quiet countrysides, fireplaces and autumn woods. He liked life orderly and people casual, their emotions properly controlled by the all-important laws of going after what one wanted purposefully. He had a way of classifying all problems and dismissing them if they did not fit his textbook formulas. Intellectual ecstasies of creating certainly weren't for him, although he found a definite pleasure, a knowledge of intrinsic values, in a Rembrandt hung above an antique mantelpiece, and enjoyed the intelligent organization of Bach. But he was not one to fling his mind wide to the elements, let them flail his soul and send him trembling feverishly to record, in words or music or in paint, his anguish or his ecstasy. It was like taking off one's clothes in public. The spirit needed intelligent companions, yes, and even a few geniuses did no great harm, but genius morning, noon and night . . .

Helen had been a genius, people said. Half the conquest had been the thrill of possessing someone much sought-after. The possession had hardly equaled the proud moment when he saw their names linked publicly . . . or the exciting moment posed for the photographers as they left the theater, or the admiration on men's faces when they went dancing — at first, when she still danced so exquisitely.

Compared to Helen, Mathilde had lacked all grace, but Helen was too intense. James was often sorry he had come to Hawaii, but Brassfield's offer to pave the way had sounded too good to a young doctor struggling in New York. . . . Brassfield had noticed Helen first, James suspected, and for that reason consulted James about his pet stomach ulcer. Helen had given James a terrible few moments when she flatly refused Brassfield's timidest advances the first week end they were invited to Lanakai. . . . James sighed. The island practice was lucrative, but on the mainland Helen might have found herself, regained her self-control or whatever it was she'd lost with her artistic career. They might not have had to be so close to one another.

The curio dealer had followed them to the door of his shop, and bowed them into the street, whipping his glasses on and off his nose in great gestures of pleasure.

"*Tsai chien*," James nodded mechanically, accomplishing the exact tone with the ease of a born Mandarin.

"*Tsai chien*," Helen mumbled miserably, unable to manage the proper tone. She wondered what the dealer thought, after they had gone. Did he laugh or shrug? She caught her mind weaving stories. Everywhere she went she tried to belong, hoping that someday there would be a door opening, then closing behind her. She wished she could have stayed behind to see what went on when

Huan locked his shop and joined his family in the back room.

There was the singsong hum of elderly men, their quiet laughter. Huan had opened his books to figure, when a sudden hearty knock at the shop door brought him out again.

"Hiya, Huan!"

Mr. Huan unlocked the door once more and four young *haole* defense workers pushed in. "Schooltime!"

"Come in. Come in." Mr. Huan was beaming. He poured them tea as they clustered around him. "I teach you Mandarin — you go China after war — "

"And get plenty rich!"

Mr. Huan shrugged. "And build new China, no?"

Instead of being hidden in a camphor chest as the shop door tinkled shut, Helen and James were swept along the street. The crowds flowed around them, hot and noisy, evil-smelling. A gust of wind from the Pali bore hints of ginger and carnations. The slick strong smell of fish and tar and ships from the waterfront curled over them. It was an insufferably hot night.

Down at the docks the white luxury liners rode

at anchor, towering above the buildings, glistening against the blue-black ocean. Out Waikiki way the hotels were filled, but not overflowing, with winter tourists dutifully eating fish and *poi*, and surf riding in the moonlight, while innkeepers complained the ridiculous war scare kept many potential travelers home.

Everywhere were the strange faces: Dandified grandsons of Moros, animated antique-ivory chessmen from Asia. Slim, quick Japanese. Pale *haoles*. The round smooth faces and patient eyes of the Koreans and Chinese.

Christmas was coming, a booming, lavish season. Europe's hard luck brought defense dollars rolling in. Overhead were Christmas lights and on the lamp posts were cardboard Santa Clauses dripping with snow. The Polynesians stared and laughed.

Helen and James pushed their way along King Street to Fort and turned left, *mauka*, towards the hills. James protested every step, hot and disgruntled, loathing the very sight of the shops.

"Merry Christmas!" He mopped his forehead, and pulled at the strangling noose of his tie. He shoved his way with growing irritability toward a counter in Kress's that was littered with Christmas wrappings. "I wouldn't be caught dead in here if you hadn't — if it weren't for you!" he crabbed to Helen, glancing uneasily about for germs.

But Helen was listening to hired carolers hidden behind a huge gilt cross and an embankment of holly. Japanese, Chinese, Filipino carolers; hearing them greet the Holy Birth in their jumbled gonglike voices.

God rest ye mer-ry gen-tle-men, let noth-ing ye dismay-e . . .

"Hello there!" A face they recognized bent toward them smiling, and then vanished behind a giant Chinese-Portuguese. The face popped in view again, a flushed, likable countenance.

Above thy deep and dreamless sleep, the silent stars go by . . .

"Hello, Jim — Helen, doing your Christmas shopping early?"

"Jerry — Sue, hello!"

Naval Lieutenant Marshall beamed down at Helen. His face had handsome large features, dark brows and friendly eyes. Sue was with him, bright, well-formed in spite of pregnancy, her hair, skin, eyes richly colored. She gave the impression of inner health, a rosy-cheeked child ready to chuckle.

"Nothing like the press at Kress!" she winked at Helen, having sized up James's mood. "We were hoping we could tiptoe in and out again unnoticed!" She ducked her head in laughter.

"So was James — but now he's trapped. He'll never forgive me, Sue — but *everyone* else is all sold out of wrappings!"

"How are you, Sue?" James bent toward her frowning.

"Jerry, Jr., and I are fine, James, but dreadfully crowded!" She disappeared behind a towering Hawaiian who, with innumerable offspring, was sauntering slowly down the aisle, clogging it.

"Jerry — " Then she bobbed free from the wave of clamoring children. She laughed disarmingly and still smiling slipped back in the tide of shoppers.

The carolers:

Silent night, holy night . . .

"You're as beautiful as ever, Helen. . . . Sue! Come here! Hey, that's my wife — " Laughing, Jerry thrust his arm deep in the crowd, fishing for Sue in the wave of human bodies.

Ho-ly in-fant so-o ten-der and mild . . .

James turned to admire Helen, for Jerry's admiration acted like a hypo, rousing him to her. He had the disturbing yet pleasing notion that Jerry might find Helen too tempting. Though Sue was sweet, Helen went deeper. Then James caught the glint of electric lights in Susan's hair and cursed himself for having married darkness.

Sleep in heav-en-ly pea-ce . . . Slee-eep in heavenly . . .

Jerry was squeezing Sue's elbow, and whispering in her ear, "Say 'good-by.'"

"I'm coming to see you soon, Helen. I'm dying to learn how you made those cunning booties for Jane Brassfield's niece. Did you crochet them? Knitted! Really? They were so-o lovely!" Sue waved.

"I'll show you . . . they were so simple. Do come!" Helen waved.

The carolers behind the cross began:

It came upon a midnight clear . . .

Jerry shook his finger at them. "You won't be lording it over us long — wait till we have our son and heir! You won't be the only parents . . ."

"And don't forget our party Saturday, will you, Sue?"

The carolers:

> . . . angels bending near the earth . . .

"Forget a party! Not the Marshalls — no, never!" Then the little bubble of white faces burst in the seething press of peoples.

≈≈≈≈

"There it is again," the Chaplain was saying, "hear it?"

Helen strained to hear, and Jacqueline, standing beside her, tiptoed anxiously. Smiling, Helen nodded. Again that indifferent social gesture after her sudden laughter. The Chaplain pondered. He had heard tales of a stricken dancer. So this was the ambitious woman Dr. Marin had taken for his second wife! He'd heard plenty of gossip at the time Mathilde died, that James was infatuated with some dancer. It had seemed a cheap and dirty lie. He had never believed it of James.

He tried to see through the fog, but it was like a wall in front of his face. The light was blurred, diffused. The air was cold and wet, but there was no wind. He barely distinguished Jacqueline who had wandered to the rail listening for the foghorns from the mainland. He saw only a brown object with golden hair, like two running blobs of water color on wet paper. He turned again to Helen, who listened eagerly, wanting to be polite. The wisps of her hair sprang up, alive, and blended into the fog. Her face was pale, pinched and cold. She was shivering unconsciously in spite of the bulky smart coat she wore. A blur of purple scarf vibrated at her throat.

Here with the fog surrounding them they stood in an enchanted time. The Chaplain felt drawn to age-old legends. Had the morning in Eden been misty when Adam awoke minus a rib? Had it been morning at all? His memory failed him! Certainly after meeting Helen Marin no one could criticize James's taste. Her strange green eyes flashed through the fog, with illness painted dark around them. A Greek mask put on for tragedy . . . And her spirited hair! But the inside of her worried him, roused him spiritually, her apparent absence of interest in her immediate danger. Was it sincere or play-acting? Why, of all people, sick and lame, was she on deck laughingly braving the fog?

≈≈≈

"We're going to explore the Point," James had tossed the remains of his sandwich to a hungry spider crab, and tapped Jacqueline's shoulder. "Come on, Jackie."

Helen yawned and lay back in the sand. "I'm too lazy." James's head jerked up as his lips spoke sympathy and his eyes exasperation.

"Of course; mind if we go?"

"Shoo!" Helen waved at them. "Go away."

The island lay stretched behind her, towering jagged cliffs thrust perpendicular from the flat of the ocean surface. All was green, bilious, violent green, except where a plow or a road slashed through and turned up scarlet earth.

Helen closed her eyes longing for the faint hues of the mainland. The watery violet of California mountains, the gray-green sage, the beige and ivory desert. She was weary of the splendor of Oahu, weary of green and scarlet and royal blue.

She raised herself on one elbow and squinted after James and Jacqueline clambering over the rocks. . . . The Point lay at the northwest tip of Oahu. To the southeast the beach curved for some miles, bordering first a golf course and then a wild strip of impassable underbrush. Offshore the sunken coral reef banded the island. Beyond the beach, right up to Kahuku Point itself, the shore became a jutting impregnable fortress built of a prehistoric lava flow. Scarcely a self-respecting crab, and but a few small shells, lived on the black rock. The gorgeous iridescent Cephalopoda and Mollusca, for which the seas were famous, roamed offshore on the reef.

It was on the beach southeast of the Point that Helen and James spent their lonely week ends before the war, far from Honolulu and its sprawling disorder. For swimming the beach was *kapu,* rough with undertow and often alive with the violet puffs and threadlike tails of the poisonous "men-of-war." There the whimsical ocean current tossed glass balls on the shore, floats from the nets of Japanese fishermen.

Helen scraped diligently with her fingernail, cleaning a glass ball and admiring the pale bubbly green glass that began to emerge from the years' growth of algae. James always cleaned them quickly and efficiently, standing in the surf, rubbing them with sand. Shuddering, Helen picked a particularly large and poignant-looking barnacle from its mooring and flung it back in the sea, hoping, as she did so, it would find another home.

"What are you doing?" James folded his long legs under him and crouched in the sand beside her, only too eager, she knew, to clean the ball for her.

"I'm feeling sorry for the barnacles."

"Why?" he looked intently at the ball, as if he expected a tenant barnacle to stretch out its neck and complain. "They have very inferior nervous systems, you know. There are millions of them." He picked one off, and with slim probing fingers began to examine it.

"Don't."

"Oh, all right." He flushed at her rebuke. "But they don't feel the way we do. They aren't exactly of the higher orders." He brushed his hands on his hips and sprang up. Then, to console her, noticing the darkening sadness in her eyes, "There are millions and millions and millions of barnacles anyway."

Helen shook her head. He was gone, zigzagging down the beach like a dog, intent on the prizes the waves had left on the shore that morning. Helen continued to scrape, frowning. She knew about nerves, and recalled, suddenly, the horror of paralysis. She stretched her legs in front of her in the sun. They really didn't show their weakness except high above her shorts on her thighs, where the scars were deep. They would serve her well

enough as an adult human content to walk. . . .
Only to walk when she wanted to dance?

Sadly Helen turned her head and followed James's steps down the sands. She admired the square of his shoulders, the calm absorption of his face as he bent to examine some secret Jacqueline unfolded in her hand. Helen could hear him promising to classify it by looking in a book when they went home. He would repeat the Latin name, Cypraeidae or Triviidae, and lay it aside — satisfied. There were books and plates, games and toys, to answer all his queries. There were none to answer hers. Helen shook her head, brushed her hand across her eyes, and remembered, with an intensity that brought tears, the poor damned barnacle floating in the surf.

"Fool!" she dug a little hole in the sand with her finger, but it filled again. "I can still imagine . . ." She lay back, her arm across her face.

She dreamed she no longer walked, but climbed with the sun across the sky, raced with the trade winds and dropped with the rain into the heaving ocean. Motion . . . motion . . . Even the sharp black jut of lava leaning against the sea moved imperceptibly, edging forward age after age until, at a given moment, which might be mathematically calculated to the remotest decimal were all the factors known, it would overstrain its cantilever, break and drop into the ocean, only to continue its motion within its core, expanding and contracting to the sun and night. All was motion, and it was in this very motion of all things that Helen found herself as she lay outwardly rigid, withdrawn into the center of her body. Her limbs were weighted with weariness, her face hardened into a sad mask, trying to hide the turmoil stirring within her.

The wind ruffled her hair. The waves of water fell back and were scooped up into a curling crystal sheet that shattered on the beach under the stress of conflicting impulses. Her dream broke with the waves.

There was only the motion of ambulances and stretchers left. Lying flat upon the sand was like lying on an operating table. . . . There was James . . . she felt his presence penetrating the veils of succeeding impressions to a night in a restaurant. She had been dancing with him. Slowly and painfully, one short dance, and then the long rest over their wine. If it hadn't been for James . . .

Helen opened her eyes and peered out between her shading fingers. There was James. She smiled, stretched out her arm and drew him close to her.

He embraced her, lying in the sand beside her, careless of Jacqueline's curiosity.

"You've been asleep."

"I've been into the midst of a nebula and hurled back. I have been . . . James, everything moves, doesn't it?"

"Umm. Yes, naturally — in a way — "

"When did *you* discover that?"

He grinned. "In school. I believe I was the only one to make an A under old Dr. Bryancamp. . . . Bill Smith told me after that exam — "

Helen interrupted him. "In school! But do you *feel* it move?" She propped herself on her elbows and peered anxiously into his face.

James pretended not to hear her, but strained a handful of sand through his fingers. This was a common thought-pattern of hers: motion, dancing, sickness. Now that she could no longer act physically her mind ran amok. It made him uneasy. She must be made to forget, to stop daring to explore man's motives. It seemed to him she was forever ripping the mental bandages of social conformity from everyone she met in order to examine them. He decided she must be made to stop trying to change the whole course of man's existence by thinking. Sometimes he wondered, if she could have had children — would it have made a difference? He thought not. She had begged to risk it at one time, but he had said no, thinking how Jacqueline already stood between them.

Helen had murmured, at the hospital, as they went guiltily from a party toward the delivery room and Mathilde, "Aren't men lucky? . . . Minerva sprang from the brain of Jove, didn't she?" He couldn't remember, there in the doorway, hearing his wife screaming with the child of a love that was already finished.

"Go in! Go . . ." Trembling and pale, Helen had pushed him. He had tried to turn back.

"Helen . . ."

Later, when it was all over, Mathilde dead and his marriage thus concluded, Helen again came wandering down the slippery path of her thoughts: "Perhaps Jove was schizophrenic . . ."

. . . James picked up a flat stone and skimmed it across the waves. Helen laughed and after a quick search produced another stone for him.

"James, what are you thinking about — me?"

"Yes, idiot, in a way. . . ."

She sensed his desire to avoid the subject. How often she had caught him building sturdy walls around unpleasantness, like the good worker he was. Entombing the intruder into his hive in wax.

"*How* are you thinking about me, James?"

He bent over and kissed her. "Never mind, idiot, I still love you." He did not smile, but took careful aim, squinting at the glittering ocean, and let the skimmer fly.

Helen sat up, tossing her hair back from her forehead, and gazed contentedly about her.

≈≈≈≈

No, the Chaplain decided. Mrs. Marin was not play-acting. It was something deep inside her that seemed to plunge forward with joyful recognition toward danger — even death. Perhaps the nearness of death before had reassured her. He spoke up, anxious to seem agreeable.

"Those are the foghorns sounding out of San Francisco."

As Helen nodded, from out of nowhere came a great cowlike moan.

"Oh, Gawd!"

They turned, startled, peering into the fog for the voice. A little Ozark woman, wife of a Honolulu bartender, had shuffled around the corner in time to hear the Chaplain's words. She seemed to joggle into homely focus as she bore forward. Tumbling after were three wooly, dirty babes. "Oh, Gawd," and her mouth slit the lower half of her face. "And us what was nearly home, Chaplain."

Helen Marin smiled even as she felt the impulse to ignore this walking, talking, human indecency. "Why, Mrs. Sparrow, didn't you hear what the Chaplain said? We're practically in San Francisco!"

The Chaplain knit his brows. What is this state of indifference beyond heroism? He snorted to himself: "Practically in Kingdom Come!"

"I don't see it!" Mrs. Sparrow muttered, brushing her mat of brown hair up from her distrustful eyes.

"But you do hear it!" Helen cheerfully patted the head of the youngest child. The latter let his chin drop and tipped his head dangerously far back to stare at her.

"Wal, yes'm, I hears somepin'," Mrs. Sparrow admitted, "but what that somepin' is — I cain't rightly say."

"It's the foghorn, the good friendly foghorn, Mrs. Sparrow, I promise you!"

"I hopes so. . . . I hopes . . ." Mrs. Sparrow glanced uneasily around. "Gives a body the creeps, don't it? This fog's like being nailed in yer own coffin afore yer time. . . . I'm agoin' to take the kids down to where it's warmlike." She shuffled away, then back to whisper, "You don't think they'd shoot kids, too, do you?"

Tears blinded Helen, her arm went about the thin shoulders, "Oh, no, Mrs. Sparrow, not the children — " She patted her bravely even as she remembered children maimed and dead, and Kim.

"I hopes not. . . . My Gawd, my Gawd." Mrs. Sparrow managed to grin shyly. Gathering her pups around her she disappeared into the fog.

Helen glanced at her wrist watch, then held out her hand to the Chaplain, smiling warmly. "Count on me — any time — please do!"

The Chaplain squeezed her hand gratefully. "I will. . . . Thank you."

Helen tapped Jacqueline's shoulder. "If you'll excuse us, we have the first mess in the wardroom!" And the merry sociable twinkle lit her eye again.

The Chaplain laughed. A deep, yet delightful woman! "You have caught on, Mrs. Marin! Thank you again for your helpful suggestions. Incidentally, you won't forget to join us for ice cream — you and the little girl?"

Jacqueline's lip curled as he spoke, but Helen

was vibrantly gracious. Her warmth seemed to push the fog back from where she stood. "We love ice cream, don't we, Jackie?"

"Yep." Jackie responded to the tug at her wrist.

Laughing gaily, Helen disappeared into the cabins, leaving the Chaplain to ponder, as the mists closed in again.

His lips moved silently, as a familiar phrase suggested itself:

I lay down my life, that I might take it again.
No man taketh it from me, but I lay it down of myself. I have power to lay it down, and I have power to take it again. This commandment have I received of my Father.

The Chaplain shook his head. That wasn't it. It wasn't so simple as that. He took up the verses further on:

. . . And many of them said, He hath a devil, and is made; why hear ye Him?

5

THE WARDROOM WAS A CLATTER OF MOTHERS, children and dishes. The steward, rocking a screaming infant in his arms, mopped his forehead with a dinner napkin and beamed mechanically as Helen and Jacqueline entered. He helped them dodge the first hazards of lurching waiters, rolling chairs, and walls that suddenly leaned against their shoulders. Jacqueline jerked her skirt out of the grasp of a gravy-smeared fist, and stepped squarely on a heap of mashed potato that had slithered down a tablecloth and plopped on the floor. They found Sue and Jane already eating. Sue managed casually, even with the baby cradled in one arm.

"The way you handle him, Sue, one would think you'd had five!" Jane was champing happily at celery — the first really nice celery she had eaten since Pearl Harbor.

"He has to depend on me for a long time as both parents." Sue paused to tuck him more securely into the crook of her elbow, handing him a spoon to play with. He promptly poked it in Jackie's ear.

"Hey," she gave him an affected grin.

Helen paused, the butter knife poised over the bread slowly dripping jelly. She realized this was the first time Sue had referred voluntarily to Jerry's death. Her heart felt lighter.

"There may be lots of things he'll have in life, but the most" — Sue swallowed — "most important thing — his Daddy — he won't have . . . But . . ." She gazed steadily at Jane with a deep glow of sympathy that caused Jane to salt her celery copiously and chew it vigorously; this distraction failing her, she fumbled for her cigarettes as Sue said, ". . . I'll have *him*."

Jane disappeared behind a cloud of smoke and began arguing loudly with the waiter over the temperature of the soup. She shook her head furiously, "The soup is cold!" After all, she told herself, Sue had somehow to support that baby, while she, Jane, had more money than old King What's-his-name. And suddenly, with her feeling of the moment, Jane decided to shower the new babe with gold. It would help armor him against subversive influences, against the rumormonger who would tell him — in the guise of a college professor, no doubt — that his father had died defending the Brassfield Enterprises of the Pacific. . . . She'd buy him a tricycle, and a dog, a big friendly dog. Her cup of sentiment slopped over as she pictured the baby tumbling after a neat Irish setter. She sniffed and blew her nose. There'd be summer camps and a car and college. . . . "George, this may well be a navy transport — but the soup is terrible." She coughed to attract attention.

"I'm sending him to Harvard, Sue," she grinned, indicating the baby with her celery, "in exactly seventeen years."

"Oh, Jane!" Sue let her teaspoon drop on her plate. The baby grabbed it and beat Jackie's arm, the one with which she was guarding her ear.

"Aw, go . . ." she handed him her spoon, too, so that he had to puzzle out the problem of holding on to three.

Helen put down her teacup with an involuntary shudder. At last. The price of Jerry Marshall's life was set — and cheap at that. Brassfield Enterprises had spent as much, quarterly, on advertising as Jane would spend in a lifetime of gifts showered on Jerry's baby.

Helen stabbed angrily at her salad, but kept her peace, as Sue thanked Jane with tearful promises of everlasting gratitude.

It had not been Jerry's death, nor the death of half her son's shipmates, that roused Jane. She'd said, "Thank God, Jack's safe!" It had taken more than Sue's hysteria and Helen's nerves, to touch her. . . . The war had finally taken Jack Brassfield like anyone else. Before that, Jane had been as one asleep in broad daylight.

Jack didn't die until Midway. She wouldn't have left the Islands if it hadn't been for that. Now . . . Well, *what* now? Jane stormed at the waiter, "If you can't bring me *hot* soup, I don't want any!"

≈≈≈

Shortly after Pearl Harbor, Jane Brassfield had decided to take Sue in hand. The poor girl had been at such loose ends since Jerry was killed, even the baby hadn't made much difference. He was such a small lump of life to replace Jerry.

Jane had steered her charge through the door of the most exclusive little dress shop in Waikiki.

"New clothes, Sue, new girl! Oh, I don't mean how you look — it's the feel of it. . . . Of course, with your figure bulging in all the wrong places — but you'll get back to normal. In fact, you've lost too much on your neck and arms already — with me it was my hips. Never went down . . . I bumped all over the floor, but it didn't . . ." Jane paused to finger with a leathery paw the fabric in a smart blue play frock. She dropped the dress with a shudder, "Sleazy . . . How in hell are we going to endure the duration without linen?"

Sue sat down upon a tiny chair and the pain inside her eased a little. She wished she weren't so tired and ill. The doctor had warned her to stay home, but she couldn't! It was lonesome there. The baby, still in his incubator, wasn't even hers yet. She answered Jane quietly. "I don't need much to wear on the boat. I don't care how I look, Jane. I'll need something warm." She smiled wryly as a salesgirl stepped forward and listened attentively. "I need a coat. I gave the one I used to wear on the mainland to — to Bundles for Britain!" The salesgirl took this as her cue. A moment later she came in dangling three coats.

"Helen said that two of James's patients who

have been evacuated told her they intended to wear slacks," Sue went on, rather sadly, not caring what she said, but not wanting to remember anything.

Jane Brassfield nodded. "That's the right idea. For the duration I'm going Spartan, slacks — straight skirts. Y'know, Sue, war *is* hell!"

Sue resented being told that, now, with her slim hard Jerry buried in the Nuuanu Valley Cemetery under lacy tree-ferns and frail bending shower-trees, blanketed by the soft thick Japanese moss that grew so ironically green over his grave. He had hated the tropics, and now for eternity . . . She fixed her eye on a bright print and slowly swung her mind back to the pursuits of shopping. Jane Brassfield was striding about the shop, thumbing the sweaters, pulling and rumpling the dresses as she held them up to her massive frame then discarded them on the nearest counter or chair.

"Try this, Sue. It's not white, but in these times, old girl, it hardly matters," and she flung a bright blue jacket into Sue's lap.

Sue stroked it thoughtfully. She liked blue. Jerry had loved it on her. Now he couldn't see it, and in spite of herself she couldn't help feeling an angry senseless pang that Jerry had gone off and would never come back. She bit her lip remembering the months when he was on sea duty and she was on the shore of the nearest port waiting. The last time he'd been shipped out for five months, then home for two weeks before December 7. . . . Sue tried on the jacket and eyed herself in the mirror, turning slowly. "I'll take it." Jerry, Jerry! You did hate black, my darling!

Jane Brassfield poured out a steady stream of gossip. She complained about her husband and the plump brown girl with the dark shy eyes he kept in a tiny cottage in Kalihi. She worried Sue about her sick dogs, too, in that congested voice punctuated by her nervous barking cough.

"Speaking of dogs, Sue, and that dog J. B. Brassfield — James Marin reminds me of a cocker spaniel!"

"James? Oh, he's a dear — so's Helen — "

"Helen's got no more appreciation of him than a Jap!"

"I guess Helen doesn't know what it is to be without — " Sue caught herself. There! She had nearly spilled over again. She shook her head. "I had a hard time getting a nurse. If James hadn't helped me cut some red tape — and Helen came down and scrubbed everything on her hands and knees!" A yellow-haired salesgirl had brought the jacket packed in a smart box.

Outside, they picked their way along the sidewalk among the soldiers and sailors. Jane flagged a taxi.

Downtown Honolulu was jammed with men in uniform, fresh from home, clustered about the theater entrances, milling in and out of curio shops and taking desperate chances on pinball machines, hunting everywhere for women.

"Naturally, I feel sorry for Helen in a way. Jacqueline's pretty sick. But with James caring for her, Helen hasn't any real worry," Jane paused to peer between the strips of tape protecting a plateglass window from shattering during an air raid, to admire a devastating hat.

She tore herself away. "I don't see why Helen keeps that filthy cat — Black Pete — he hasn't any pedigree. Cats are dirty beasts, likely as not to carry typhus lice — especially if they catch those horrible plague rats."

"Wouldn't you say Helen's an — an introvert?" Sue stumbled over the word because she wasn't sure it was kind.

"That cat! My God! What can James see in

Helen? She's so —" Jane Brassfield instinctively loathed artists with a primitive fear of the unknown.

"I think James must love her," Sue said limply. She didn't know why they talked so much, on and on. She was tired, but afraid to stop and rest for fear of memories and the dread emptiness of tomorrow.

"Does he?"

Sue wavered. "Don't you think so? He seems devoted."

"He's devoted to appearing devoted. He doesn't mind the credit. It's that very devotion that makes James impossible. We all have our blind spots, and I suppose that's his. It's what makes it possible for most females to find a gullible male — even a spavined dancer like Helen!"

"She covers it skillfully enough — she's very attractive," Sue felt on safer ground. Helen was pretty.

"Sure. Oh, and I dare say she's much sicker than she admits. . . . But did you know — you'd never guess — she's not even thirty! James said 'poor dear Helen' fainted after the first air-raid alarm. Silly nervous creature . . ."

"I saw her yesterday. She was terribly upset over

Jacqueline, and now she thinks James will be called up. She says he's all she has."

"I don't see why she doesn't take an active part in charities."

"She's not very strong — and she is studying to be a Nurses' Aide."

"Hah!" Jane snorted. "That! And you, too, Sue, you're not doing anything constructive — " Jane blundered to a stop.

"No, Jane, I'm not doing anything."

"I'm sorry, Sue. Here's the Young bar, let's — " Jane floundered to escape and went in deeper. "Hell, Sue, I didn't mean to talk about Jerry."

"Jane," Sue's voice was thin and dry, "we're downtown to have — lots of fun. Let's forget it — "

In spite of Sue's plea Jane couldn't forget. "But that is what's wrong with you, Sue, you need to take a good grip — "

"Let's not talk about it, Jane."

"Now there you are! It's people like you, Sue, who have to wake up . . . come out of your shell . . . fight back. Jerry died for a better world — for a white man's Christian world!"

"Jane." Sue stopped dead in the street facing her. "As far as I'm concerned the war's over. Finished. I don't want to hear about it. Can't you understand that I don't give a damn, Jane, what kind of a world we live in? It just doesn't seem to matter any more!"

Jane Brassfield gasped. The charity button on her bosom flashed in the sun. Sue didn't give her a chance to answer. She ran, pushing against soldiers, stumbling over curbs, sobbing for the first time since Jerry died, sobbing out loud in front of God and everybody, aching and wondering if her insides were going to fall right out of her.

≈≈≈≈≈

Jane scraped the last spoonful of ice cream, smiling at Sue, who smiled back. "Harvard in seventeen years!" she beamed. A foghorn groaned dismally.

6

THE CRUISER ESCORT HOVE TO AT DUSK AND LAY off the starboard bow. Muffled fog-choked voices gave orders, answered them. Along the passageways the listeners chattered helplessly.

"They've located a sub."

"Can't go in — channel's mined —"

"Orders are to put out to sea again, cruise tonight, and make port when and if the fog lifts in the morning."

"Good God! To sea again!"

"If this were peacetime, they'd charge extra for the cruise."

" 'Cruise-ify' — huh?"

"Notify all passengers of the alert — tell them to stay with their children at all times!"

"Yes, sir."

In the wardroom, after dinner, sat several officers and the few females who were not attached to children and who looked calmly and with amusement on all the harried women who were. There was a gaiety aboard ship, a hectic nervousness drowned by gales of laughter and deep-voiced bravado. Helen wandered along the corridors that were within bounds. Below decks — out of bounds to women evacuées — lay some of the wounded who had survived the battle of Midway. Down there was heat and rolling seasickness and pain — and the defenders of civilization.

But for the darkening of the gray into black, and the bosun's whistle measuring the hours, there was no time.

Jacqueline gasped and coughed in the stuffy cabin and eyed the porthole longingly. As the lights were on, it was necessary to seal it for the night.

Blackout was normal to her life. It was no longer frightening or unfamiliar to prowl about the dark like primitive tribesmen. The dark was rather friendly. Perhaps electricity wasn't so important after all, nor the invention of gunpowder, nor the steam engine. Whatever it was that made older people speak optimistically about the future Jacqueline had no share of it. She did not have faith in anything any more.

Jacqueline turned in her bunk and covered her face with her hands. She suffered secretly, in doubting fear of people, full of uncertainty. She was like a swift stream at the mercy of a high and narrow gorge, plunging over waterfalls, down into the dark regions under the earth and up again, battered over rocks and cleaved by stumps, pouring at last into the monstrous swelling anonymity of the sea.

≈≈≈

"Kim — Kim — " she had whispered from her bedroom window the night of the Marins' party. "Can you see them necking?"

Kim nodded, and motioned to her to join him. He was grinning. He proffered one of a fistful of bonbons. "Hi, Jacqueline!"

"Hi," she had breathed, crouching beside him in her thin nightgown. "It's cool out here. . . . Move over a little. I want to peek."

Kim made room for her. Her gown was pulled taut from her neck to her knees as she knelt to peer through the ferns and bamboo. The soles of her feet were black with loamy earth. She wiggled her toes excitedly as she giggled.

"Polly Ling is kissing Dr. Wong. . . . Gee, look at them!" She nudged Kim. "There's old man Brassfield drunker than . . . Ooooh, here comes Daddy. . . . Come on!"

Silently they fled the garden, their bare feet gripping the moss and their lean bodies thrusting through broad-leafed plants and thorny undergrowth of rangy weeds. They found the steps leading up the heights and raced up two at a time. Exhausted they sank down in a bed of moss hidden by hibiscus and huge leaves of taro.

"*Sssh*, hear the music." Kim pressed Jackie's arm. "I can see the lights on the *lanai*."

"That's the guest bedroom," Jackie corrected. She pulled her nightgown away from her body, shaking it. "I'm hot now." She was still panting. Kim put his arm around her.

"I made you run too fast," he said kindly, and for once she did not protest. From the hilltop they looked out on the gay lights of the battle fleet lying at anchor in Pearl Harbor and beyond, at the solid endless blackness of the surrounding ocean. They felt wonderfully alive, watching the twinkling of lights, feeling their hearts beating. The night gave to the ocean an appearance of friendly complicity, as if, being precious living things, they were kept snugly hidden in the depth of a gigantic black velvet box. In their ears the deep tones of frogs and the higher notes of crickets almost drowned the music of the party. Overhead, trade clouds passed swiftly beyond the triangular flaps of taro leaves. Kim picked a hibiscus and stuck it through the ribbon eyelets of Jackie's nightgown, between her tiny breasts.

"Oh, Kim, you shouldn't. . . ." Jackie felt his hands cup her breasts; lifting her hands she put them over his, and lay still smiling.

At last she whispered, "Let's take off our things — just for fun." She felt so close to whatever the core of living was that clothes and houses had seemed suddenly meaningless.

"All right," Kim whispered. Leaping to his feet he stripped and stood before her. His body was soft and young and very clean. Jacqueline jerked her nightgown over her head and threw it on the ground. She did not feel shy at all. She reached out and stroked Kim's skin. It was silken, like her own.

They did not speak, so new and wonderful was this final step into maturity. Kim's fingers dug the rich black earth and pressed it into her hands. They stood together, their heads tipped back, breathing the warm moist air and watching the stars blink out from behind the clouds. The feeling of life was pulsing everywhere in the blackness.

"Oahu — island of Oahu —" Kim spoke it softly as a bird call.

Far down below them washed the sea, and underfoot was the warm steamy earth-mother giving life to abundant plants and crawling creatures. Jackie laid her bare arm next to Kim's. In the faint light of the stars they were the same color. Swiftly and gently their hands explored each other. Laughing silently they wrestled on the moss, until without a hint of warning Jackie screamed a long and frantic, "Ooooh . . ." Kim's skin chilled as he leapt back.

"A *buffa* — a *buf-fa!*" Jackie was on her feet, fleeing down the hill, white and naked, her hair streaming out behind her.

Kim clutched her nightgown in his hands. Beside him in the bushes he heard a sluggish rustle and out came an enormous toad, loathsome and fat, his big eyes bulging and his hideous mouth agrin. Kim cried out, falling against the earth. The great frog only blinked where he squatted, as the sobbing boy buried his face in the cool moss, his fingers digging the sod.

Twenty-four hours later, with their world shattered, their friends dead and dying, Jacqueline had heard Helen say, "It is immoral. . . ." That was the first night of blackness, when the island lay devastated after the battle. Jacqueline lay in the bedroom, staring at the ceiling. She had been crying.

Helen poured James another cup of coffee. In ten minutes he must return to the hospital. Wong had offered to take over, when he heard of the bombing on the heights. On finding Helen safe, James had demanded food.

"What's immoral? The way I eat?" He glanced at her from under black lashes and the sanity in his weary eyes cheered her soul.

"To turn out the lights. It isn't as if we were ignorant and had no way of lighting the dark. But to return to darkness! That is sin!"

"Sin?" James poured the cream and stirred it about in his coffee. He was listening with but one ear, the other was inverted, hearing again the morning raid, listening to the mutilated men, the cries for guns. He remembered one man beating on the door with both his fists. The ammunition was locked up, someone had misplaced the key, something had gone wrong . . . Helen was continuing to expand her thoughts:

"Ignorance is not sin, and to act through ignorance is not sin, but it seems to me that the intelligent, the so-called informed, well, for example, the white man. . . . In God's name what are we doing to the earth?"

"The white man! What about the yellow men! For God's sake, Helen, you're always talking, talking . . . Immorality — sin . . . Oh, what the hell!" He found relief in turning on her.

Helen shrugged. "That's what I'm driving at. *We* should have known. Intelligent, enlightened people that we claim to be."

"Oh, nuts!" And James threw back his head in an extravagant gesture, so handsome that Helen's heart leaped. He looked straight into her eyes. His were scornful, angry and tired.

Suddenly she laughed. "Could you eat another sandwich?" She pushed the plate toward him. What was she doing, anyway, philosophizing, wailing? It was a secondary place, standing behind a man of action, but it was a place — a foothold on sanity. "Darling?"

"Butter . . . Is there any more butter? Oh, and bring me a piece of cheese — a good slice — and mustard."

Helen brought them. "And you a doctor! How can you eat that stuff?" She sat down once more at the table, resting her chin on her hands, and stared at him. She admired his regular, self-assured features. Then she thought of Kim — and Jacqueline. How could Jackie have turned on her friend, as if he were suddenly a personal enemy? Helen shivered, remembering the morning, the unleashing of unreasoning hate. It had been a peculiar feeling to wake and find oneself the target, to be shot at and violated before one's own temper was aroused. . . . Helen decided to explain to Jackie that hate must not be allowed to hit back at the innocent. That settled, Helen glanced again at James, then at his hands. Thank God, he still had them both. These were the sickening hours — after the battle — when one remembered and wondered. But for the grace of God it might have been . . . This was the time of terror after the danger. But, Helen reminded herself in amazement, this was not only recollection of danger past, this was realization of danger faced. What of tomorrow, and tomorrow . . . ? James's voice broke through her thoughts; apparently he had been speaking for some time.

". . . The best place would be in the house, against an interior wall. Unless there is a direct hit you'll be all right. I'll be away all night, but if anything should happen — "

"The invasion? It may come." She spoke steadily as she looked out and watched the dusk descending on the town and harbor. The dark spread like ink through a blotter until she could hardly see James's face. She followed the outline of it, sharp and even against the sky where red clouds like bubbles of blood were rising out of the western ocean, out of Japan.

"Follow the valley up into the hills — not the Nuuanu, that's too well known, and strategic — but over in Pauoa, into the wilderness. You could live for weeks if you had food."

"And you?" She was wondering if this could really be the continuation of their world. Their little world that last night talked of love and Brassfields and quarreled some . . . They had not been lovers, but had crept to bed, their stomachs hollow and their heads aching.

"I'll come when I can." James shook out a cigarette and then, remembering the blackout, poked his head under the tablecloth to light it.

"It's funny how quickly one adapts oneself." Helen watched him come up for air, then plunge under the table for another drag. "Today I remembered to lie flat on the floor when the bomb came."

"What about Jackie — did she duck, too?"

"I nearly broke her arm pulling her down. She was paralyzed with horror. . . . And then, after that, she said such vile things to Kim . . . Poor Kim — will he die, James?"

"No. . . . But good God! Helen, why shouldn't she call him names?"

"But, James, to talk like that to someone who was hurt . . ." She caught an amused flicker in his eye. No, he didn't understand her.

"You have always fought reality, and now — along comes a war, and you stand right up and thumb your nose at it!"

"James, darling, I love you . . ."

He caught her hand hastily, laughing, and rose. "Not tonight, my pet! Good-by. . . ."

She felt the smile freeze on her lips and retorted primly, "No, naturally not!" She watched him vanish into the shadows of the garden walk.

"Jacqueline!" There was no answer. "Jacqueline, come — out here, please." Jacqueline came sullenly. "We have a night to face together — dear." Even in the dusk, Helen caught a spark from Jacqueline's eyes, like a hammer striking steel.

"Yes, Mo-ther."

≈≈≈≈≈

"Mother?" Jackie hung over the edge of her bunk. The skin was milky blue over her breastbone, the cords in her neck taut.

"Mother, how can we sleep tonight when we're going to dock tomorrow? Jeepers! San Francisco! I'm so excited . . ."

She rested her chin on her hand with a sigh. Suddenly she was sick and lonely. So long as they were at sea, there was a link between her and the Islands. When they docked it would be broken. She longed for Ahulani with sudden hot tears. She longed for a song or a story told in the dusk to the rustling of coconut palms and the surge and crash of waves. Some of the stories were mysterious and sad. There was the one of the turbulent waters where people died and their voices called for others to come join them. That was the way they said Kim's mother had died. . . . Perhaps Kim, too . . . Jacqueline sighed again, wistfully: she could not remember people on the mainland believing stories, singing songs. She missed the heavy scent of flowers through the window, the quarreling mynahs in the mango tree at dusk.

"Mother . . ."

"Go to sleep, Jackie."

"Mother, supposing something happens to us . . . these are evil waters . . ."

"No, they're not. Nothing will happen, nothing." Helen's voiced promised, but she pinned her money, her favorite valuable jewels and a box of aspirin into a flat purse and snapped it to the belt of her skirt. She told herself: Nothing will happen again in our lives — uprooted, torn apart, neither good nor evil can touch us. . . . She reached up and tucked Jackie in, as if she were still a little child; and then, unable to sleep herself, she went to the corridors to walk.

Jacqueline snuggled down, relieved, just as that first night, after the battle and personal anger, they had sat silent as Helen twisted the radio dial back and forth.

≈≈≈

The two local stations were dead, except for an occasional order to the people from the Military Governor. Martial law had been declared. Helen together, reasonably and sensibly, that afternoon of Monday, December 8. She was staring at James, who lay sleeping after working all day Sunday and all Sunday night. Sitting motionless in the bay of the bedroom, her eyes memorized the stiff blossoms of the lobster claw, the glint of blond wood against flowered linens, the cracked beige fiber of an ancient *tapa* hanging on the wall. She was trying to think ahead. Her limp hands and aching legs tingled, but she refused them any sympathy. The world was at war today.

Monday was dark and cold. A day of rains and swirling mists after the hell of Sunday. Helen shivered in her tweed jacket that still reeked of mothballs. She could not remember having worn it once since coming to the Islands. This was not a day of external cold alone, the chill seemed to come from within.

Helen unfolded the evening paper, finding momentary distraction in the amusing printer's errors. She had visions of nervous hands, all thumbs, cigarettes aslant in shouting lips. One of the advertisements had been inserted upside down.

She folded the paper neatly in her lap and sat without moving, watching the still figure on the bed breathing slowly.

Once she went to the phone for James, calling

the hospital to inquire about Kim. He was just the same, they said. She returned to the bedroom passing Jacqueline on the *lanai* engrossed in a story, eating a banana. Helen wondered how anyone but Jacqueline could eat today. Yet they had both slumped to the floor laughing hysterically at finding the cat had jumped in the refrigerator for his lunch when they weren't looking. Helen had found him with his feet in the cottage cheese, shivering and chastened. It was a day of sudden giggles of relief jerked involuntarily out of still-writhing stomachs, and muffled by gasps of apprehension.

Helen had been at work all morning planning their new life. She had taken an inventory of the pantry shelves, rearranged the medicine cabinet, and fixed a kit of first aid necessities. With the help of Jacqueline she had found cardboard to black out the panes of the bedroom windows.

Now she sat in the alcove and waited for James to wake. As she worked, she had forgotten Sunday, but now her mind kept creeping back to it. . . . This morning, when she had failed to find the fresh hibiscus which Ahulani always laid out on the piano, she had buried her face in her hands trying to blacken out the realization of death — of Joe Ferrara standing at the door, asking for Ahulani, and not finding her, wandering huge and bewildered along the island roads until sprawled in the dust at his feet he found her. . . . The tears had not come, but there had been a constriction in Helen's throat and a shock in her spine that sent her flying from the room.

Again she studied the lobster claw, vaguely aware of the telephone and Jacqueline's "Aw, nuts . . ." as she dragged herself up to answer it. The hospital was checking James's whereabouts. Helen thumbed the newspaper, rereading the ads and forgetting them.

From far down in the city, Helen heard the wail of a fire engine. She listened and then dismissed it. It came again. Suddenly a response pricked her brain. No, not fire engines any more! The alarm! The alarm! She felt her fingers sticking together, clammy and cold.

"James!" she whispered, and marveled at the composure in her voice. "The air-raid alarm! Jacqueline! Come in here! Hear it?"

James was slow to react. His aching body rejected the alarm, but Helen was shoving him into his clothes and muffling a protesting Jacqueline into a sweater, "Just in case we have to sleep out tonight."

127

James stood like a ton of clay dumped in the middle of the room. Suddenly he turned around, "I'm going back to bed . . ." And then he saw Helen, her head flung up, her eyes brilliant and alert.

"Helen . . . Have you a kit? Emergency supplies?"

"Yes, yes, everything. I have a suitcase packed. Everything. See?" Helen showed him a suitcase filled with canned stuffs: chocolate, milk, beef. There was a neat first-aid kit, a blanket, a flashlight . . . James weighed it in his hand.

"Too heavy — take out the blanket — wear more clothes." James stopped and faced Helen in amazement. "Say, when did you do all this?"

"This morning, early. Jackie helped me. We've a folding cot and an umbrella, too. No matter what happens — "

"Helen . . . If they come back — we're helpless. . . ." James hesitated. No sense alarming her. Yet if they didn't come it would be a miracle. . . . The Japs must know our unpreparedness. . . . In a few weeks perhaps help would come from the mainland. Until then . . . God help us!

Why call on God? An intangible foolishness, no more of a weapon than the budding flowers making the garden bright even on a gray day, not a gun, not a knife, not an airplane, yet . . . *Dear God, send us men, send us men* . . . James prayed shyly, fumbling with the lock on the suitcase. "Helen . . ."

"Yes?" She turned from Jacqueline and came to him, her green eyes shining bravely. This — whatever else it might be — was living, this was creating, this was meeting and thinking and acting against obstacles. This was the end of egoism. This turning to face death squarely — was living! Since yesterday morning she had moved in a state of frenzied exaltation, for her consciousness, that had been forced to walk for so long to keep pace with her body, now leaped of necessity down paths of imperative action.

"Darling, there may be an invasion — which makes me sound like a damned alarmist — but there may be. . . . We're not sure — but if — "

"Yes, James?"

"We were caught off guard yesterday, pretty badly shot up — the whole island besides Pearl Harbor: Kaneohe, Schofield, the whole works — planes — ships — flattened. . . . I saw a lot of it, and I'm not exaggerating. . . . I was . . ." James stopped, staring at her. Between them he felt a current so strong he was helpless. He put his arms around her. "Don't be afraid, Helen. . . . We'll get through this all right."

"I'm not afraid, James!" Helen shook back her curls; she smiled slowly, soberly.

"Thank God, you think it can't happen to us!"

"No," Helen's smile disappeared. "Things do happen to us. . . . Tomorrow we may be dead. Or prisoners . . . But we can try to live in the hills up high in the caves in those hidden valleys — we *can*, James; we will. You musn't worry. I'm all right."

Jacqueline was on the *lanai* peering down on the city and then toward Pearl Harbor. "Mother, I can't see a thing. I can't hear any planes either — can you?"

A flash of laughter lit James's face. "What do you want, for God's sake, Jackie, bombs?" He swung Helen around the room. "Is this really us?"

Helen clung to him, her spirits wild. Everything conspired to make this moment perfect. She brushed aside the passing intuition that it was melodramatic and cheap in the midst of war . . . and then she remembered Jacqueline. She gave James a wifely kiss on the cheek and turned to her stepdaughter, wishing the child were in school, or in the bathtub, any place but standing there loose-lipped and rabbit-eyed.

From the city below, the wail of sirens rose again, clearly whining in the dusk. James heaved a sigh of relief and collapsed on the bed.

"All clear!"

"All clear, Mother!" Jacqueline echoed, snatching off her sweater and waving it about her head, "We're safe!"

Helen felt the blood drain from her face.

James shouted to Jacqueline for water. Helen felt herself pressed against the soft mattress, the fuzz of the blanket between her fingers. Faintly she heard the quarrelsome mynahs in the mango tree on the terrace echoing, "Safe, safe, safe . . ."

≈≈≈≈≈

7

SILENTLY THE SHIPS PLOWED THE FOG AND SEA, steadily through the night. The torpedo had not come. Later perhaps. In one minute, two minutes, twelve hours, or never. . . . Helen listened at her cabin door. She heard only the swish of waves pushed back from the sides of the ship, felt only the pull of the engines through the swells. As she closed the door behind her she saw that Jane had fallen asleep on the cot set between the berths. A cigarette smoldered between her fingers. Helen took it, crushing it out.

The sealed cabins were stifling in spite of the ventilators. Jacqueline was tossing in the upper berth. Helen knew she must be miserable. She turned back to open the cabin door a crack but there came such a gust of misty air she closed it again fearing the baby would catch cold.

"Mother, it sounds like bombs," Jacqueline mumbled.

"Perhaps you have a little fever, dear, but *ssssh*" — as Sue's baby whined in his sleep — "don't wake the baby." She shaded the light away from the others.

Sue lay silent in her berth. Her body was no longer full and round but straight and childish in her pajamas. She rose on her elbow and bent over the baby. He had to sleep with her, as no bed had been provided, and at six months, the women observed sagely, he hogged the bed like any full-grown male. Sue had to prop a chair against the berth to keep from falling out as she curled around him. He was restless and cross. He coughed.

With a sighing sleepy mutter to Helen, "There he goes again, the whole darn bottle whoopsed on the blanket!" Sue bundled him off to the bathroom. She ran with the slope of the ship's flooring, cautiously bending her elbow out to protect the baby's head from striking the walls.

The strong white light of the bathroom blinded them both. The baby blinked, starting to fuss. Carefully hooking a stool with her bare toes and sitting down on it, Sue scrutinized the youngster. His mouth formed a square as he wailed.

133

Panic stabbed her. Perhaps he was ill, perhaps he was going to die! He coughed, and dribbled the last ounce of formula on his shirt. Her heart flopped over against her ribs and her stomach caved in.

Panic swept away the memory of the doctor's cheerful reassurances. How did he know the baby would survive the trip? She remembered the ghastly morning he had refused his Pablum, when the doctor said he was ready for it, and the time when nothing, nothing at all, had made him stop screaming all night long. . . . Helen and Jane were useless to her. Like all parents of grown children, Sue's anguish seemed only to amuse them. And what if he were dying now? What if he stopped breathing? Just stopped. How many times had she tiptoed in the night, afraid when he was fussing that he was dying, and when he was quiet that he was dead! Once she had even pinched him. When he woke sobbing, she'd hushed him and loved him joyously.

Fear was wrapped like strangling wet cloths around her face. Her hands were slippery with perspiration. It stood out on her forehead, and her pajamas clung to her damp skin. Shakily she began to undress and clean the child, watching every minute lest death snatch him.

She felt a pang of nausea. The acrid odor of the sick baby, the heat . . . It was too much, too much, being forever responsible, guarding her infant every moment. Sometimes she thought she couldn't stand it any longer, but she did.

Sue had been sick since the beginning of pregnancy, not seriously at first, but she had tried too hard to keep up with Jerry, to make his brief leave exciting. That first month before he was shipped out, before anyone knew she was going to have a baby, she'd been sick often and at embarrassingly unpredictable moments. There was the time of Jane's *luau*. Jerry had been crazy to go. (Sometimes Sue wondered why she still spoke to Jane, even now, after that hideous party. Yet why did Jane speak to *her*, and offer to send the baby to college?)

≈≈≈≈≈

Ancient torches had flickered against the narrow bamboo leaves. Across the soft cool lawn dancing girls swung into an old love dance, like tall palms answering the ocean winds. In the center of the lawn places were laid for sixty or eighty guests. Antique wooden bowls were filled with *poi*. There was wonderful cold salmon on *ti* leaves, crisp chunks of pineapple. . . . But the feast was devastated, the guests drunk, the dancing girls naked.

"Hallo, Sue!" A rough voice stripped her.

Sue had looked up, tired and sleepy, and only remembered at the last minute that it was her duty to smile. "Mr. Brassfield, your party's lovely!" Jerry had cautioned her to be polite to him. "I don't know how Jane finds time from all her charities to entertain so romantically," Sue plunged on, looking about for Jerry. Lord! To get away without a scene!

"Good dancing girls, too, huh?" J. B. Brassfield, his dinner jacket filthy, his red face sweaty, put his arm around her.

"Where did you find them?" Sue tried to push him away.

"I just whistled — that's all John B. has to do! J. B. beckons, and the whole island comes running — military and civilian." He mouthed the words drunkenly, bragging incautiously, "I beckon and the Navy sends a ship — I call and the Army grovels — "

"You have a fine business head!" Sue stretched her dry lips into a smile.

Mr. Brassfield beamed, tugging harder at her. He was dragging her behind the bamboo toward a banyan tree. Among the hundred trunks Sue gazed about and shuddered. The Lord had made the banyan a brothel for the rich!

"I tell you I own the island, Sue. Any little token you . . ."

Sue grew faint, her voice whispered sarcastically, "And that's what the U. S. Army and Navy are for, Mr. Brassfield! *Your* servant, sir!"

Her esophagus opened: shreds of salmon, pineapple, quantities of *poi* . . . Brassfield whirled angrily, glancing about for help. Sue had crumpled on her hands and knees at the foot of the banyan. Finally he had begun to yell, like an enraged bull.

"Jerry, hey Jerry! Your wife's drunk!"

≈≈≈≈≈

Sue had just fallen asleep again on her cot when the baby wailed and sneezed twice.

Jacqueline opened her eyes. "Mother, I want to go out on deck!"

"Go to sleep! Don't get up, Sue, this time I'll look after him." Helen took up the child.

"Oh, thanks awfully! Are you sure you don't mind?" Sue snuggled back on the berth, luxuriating for the moment in having it all to herself, even if there was a wet spot between her shoulder blades where he had lain.

Helen rested the infant across her shoulder. He clutched the sensitive hairs behind her ear in his pink moist fingers and promptly lost some more of his dinner down her neck. He blinked, smiling angelically, and belched. Even as she wiped her neck and shoulder, Helen hugged him. She had loved him from the moment Jane had called her from the hospital.

≈≈≈

Jane's voice had frightened her. Rough, blubbering, profane.

"Sue had her baby — damn near killed her — twelve o'clock last night . . . four pounds — a boy. I thought I'd call you." The voice paused for an answer, but Helen had none.

"Thank you, Jane. Give her my love." Slowly she lowered the telephone. So! The son and heir. Born prematurely on December 7 — a posthumous son.

She had not wept. Helen had wandered back into the living room. Dawn was at least two hours away. Why did it have to be Jerry — Jerry's young

138

body? Why? To the beginnings and to the ends of time why? And for what?

≈≈≈≈

In the light of the ship's bath, Helen wiped the baby's mouth. He was going to be a fine child when he filled out. He was still too thin, and not very pretty. Already he had the large features that had distinguished Jerry and given realism to his open friendly manner.

Helen wrapped the infant in a clean blanket. It was that lovely one that Jane had knitted for Sue after that awful episode in town when Sue blew up all over Fort Street. . . .

Helen tucked the pink afghan about the baby's feet. He seemed willing at last to settle down and go to sleep.

Jane had wallowed on her cot until she lay on her stomach, her slacks drawn tight and mocking across her ponderous rear. Sue had dozed. She mumbled gratefully as Helen laid the baby in her arms, switched out the light and stretched on her own bunk without undressing.

Helen lay staring into the dark. Outside the porthole lay the ocean, the fog and a submarine.

Within was the blackness of the sealed cabin. The dark pressed along her body. She heard the ship's horn lowing mournfully and the sister ships answering.

The eternal dark! Would she ever again lie down with James and find the darkness was of love, and not of stealth and danger? Viewed from her hard bunk in the boxlike cabin, the two hundred nights of blackout they had been together seemed short.

Helen needed James now. He kept her on an even keel. He lit up the shadows that lurked in the back of her mind, and kept her course straight. He had led her back from that awful moment when, as she foundered on the verge of cracking up, she had flung away the cat. There in the crowded cabin among the hot sleeping bodies, Helen began to think and to withdraw from the terrible labyrinth of darkness she wandered in, tried to find James as she groped back through the dark turns of her mind.

≈≈≈≈≈

The darkness had been nothing when they faced it together. Every night when the sun was setting, Helen had taken a long last look at the silent city, alert and armed, before she had blacked out the windows for the night and withdrawn into the innermost part of the house. On her left was Punchbowl, sharp and clear against the sky, the dead remains of an ancient volcano. Below Punchbowl the city curled against the shore. The old matchbox houses, with peeling paint and rickety balconies, leaned one against the other. The narrow winding streets were deserted except for sentries marching up and down, fingering their sleek high-powered rifles. On other nights before the war, when the city and the battle fleet had lain bejeweled with strings of lights, how the island must have sparkled on the ocean, tempting thieves from the sky. . . . Now there was darkness everywhere, darkness and the restless waiting, listening for the peculiar whine of the alarm that plunged a cold steel knife in the spine.

The total blackout was accented by the eerie flash of dim blue lights from the army trucks and occasional ambulances. Dogs barked spasmodically, and from far up the valley came the plaintive bleat of goats. To the right — Ewa way — lay Pearl Harbor and the battle-scarred ships. There was the desperate future . . . The dead past. The human dead, the dead ideals.

There had been another battle somewhere. They

had heard the roar of depth charges, seen giant flashes on the horizon. Pearl Harbor lay behind a smoke screen. It had been a big battle. First had come Java, then the Coral Sea, now this. . . . Where? No one knew. . . . Some hinted Midway.

Somewhere, far out there — so the telegram to Jane had read — Jack Brassfield had been killed in action while helping his wounded superior officer onto a life raft.

Helen drew the heavy blackout curtains carefully so that no streak of light peeped through to bring wrathful Marines pounding on the door. She lit the bridge lamp, took up her knitting and listened. Jacqueline, still convalescing from fever, had fallen asleep already. The house was silent except for clumsy noises in the kitchen, and the slam of the refrigerator door. James was in search of a drink.

Nervously, Helen dug her needle into a stitch and clacked away across a row of purling. She worked all day in the hospital and at night she knitted scarves for the men in the northern seas. She could not stop working, so imperious was her need to act, even when the pain in her legs made her face gray and her step short and jerky.

James knocked at the door, and she jumped to switch out the light. "Come in."

The door opened cautiously and James stumbled through the dark like a tall black lacquer statue, a stream of moonlight framing him. With a deft kick, he shut the door and waited while Helen once more lit the lamp. They stood blinking and smiling across the table. James held a tray of spilling wine, as Helen cleared away the litter of leisure hours. James had dragged out all the back numbers of his medical journals, but somehow the evenings usually slipped away to the monotonous drone of war news and the pursuit of a silent game of chess. Helen played an interesting game, erratic, diabolical in that it followed no recognized gambit, but started with Hitler tactics of deep spearheads and quick counterthrusts. James's game was slow, a bit British in its openings, but ponderously hard to beat. They seldom finished a game, however, as James usually had a call to take him to the hospital.

James smiled as he offered her some wine. "Remember the times when we could throw up the blinds and let the lights blaze?"

Helen nodded, wiping the glass before setting it on the table. "It's the commonplace act — the simple thing," she said, as they'd said often enough. "Remember the time when we were first married and had that microscopic apartment in New York with our priceless Rouault over the imitation fireplace? What a strange old duck Uncle Bill was to break down and give us a gift like that, after all the years he let me struggle along after Father and Mother died! Any dancing that was not chaperoned in the Civic Auditorium was not up to his Pasadena moral standard." A wicked little smile peeked out at James, then disappeared as she said, "Oh, well, he certainly liked — that is — approved of you, dear. . . ."

"Are you implying anything?"

"No. . . . And that first year after my accident — invalids are unbearable people, aren't they, James?"

"You're being incoherent." He reached to turn on the radio.

"How did you stick it out, darling?"

James put his fingers around her neck as if to strangle her. It flashed through his head that it would be easy. He was revolted, saying quickly, "Some of the old wives called it retribution, didn't they? I called it love!" He sat down feeling purged and pure.

Helen's lip curled to sneer, but she forced a smile and hastily lit a cigarette. "Thank you, dear. . . . Remember how we used to walk to the corner for a coke before going to bed, as it was all the walking I dared? . . . And some nights when you were late getting home from the hospital—"

"You went to bed thirsty," James laughed, but Helen remembered how long the hours had been, and that several times she had seen a girl drive away after leaving him at his door. Because of her sickness, because of the memory of his dead wife, because she was afraid, she had never spoken of it. Now she said, "Yes, desperately thirsty!"

She clung to his gay mood. "James, close your eyes tight — really tight, no fair peeking — can you see a hilltop in California with Los Angeles below transformed by night into a sparkling field of fairy night flowers?"

James roared, "Fairy night flowers!" He shook his head snorting. "But I remember beach parties and desert parties and *me* transformed by Scotch — good Scotch. Remember it, Helen?" He eyed his wine distastefully. It was a nondescript brand, and very sour. At least they weren't reduced to drinking saki!

"*Ummmm*, I remember," Helen put away her knitting and took up her drink.

James lifted his glass and stared through the red fluid at the light. He peered down at Helen. She had curled like a pet on the bed, laughing at him.

She made a delightful composition, her thin alert face with the shining green eyes glistening in the shadows. The sharp hook of the lobster claw in the earthen pot behind her reminded James of the stiff gestures of a Balinese dancer, while a darkened mirror, out of the light, reflected Helen's image from another point of view.

James had the strange sensation that looking at Helen and her reflection was like seeing her wild spirit whole and naked. A profound Picassoesque portrait, masked by a flippantly sophisticated presentation. Had she not often implied that she was two? The image in the glass must be the part of her that he would never understand. The Helen that raced with the trade winds and laughed down at him from dizzy pinnacles of fancy . . . among the fairy night flowers! Lord, the wine was potent!

He bent toward Helen, holding his wineglass to his eye. She was scarlet, and her eyes, the green counteracted by the intense chroma of the red, darkly brooding. Helen lifted her mouth to be kissed. It was then the two images slid into focus, merged into one desirable shape and James was no longer philosophical.

"It's been so long," Helen whispered finally, brushing a lock of hair back from his forehead.

"Too long," he murmured.

"Why . . . ?"

James did not answer her, too relaxed to utter any sound. Then in the back of his mind there came a memory.

"I love you, Helen" — but in spite of his words, the tone of his voice was like an alarm to her heart.

"I love you . . . James?"

"I — I was going to tell you earlier this evening, but — " James chuckled suddenly, and Helen knew he had returned to normal by an unknown necessity, like his response in the night to a sick call — "so far, tonight I've wanted to put it off."

"What, James, what is it?"

"The war, Helen; you know — "

Why couldn't he ever come to the point? "War?"

"Yes. Helen — it's going to involve us more than I had first thought."

Helen began to tremble. "Your commission . . ."

"Yes, it came through. . . . You and Jacqueline will be evacuated immediately to the mainland. You'll wait there for me until . . . You'll be safe there . . ."

"Oh!" James heard the cry rise in her throat, low and guttural with pain. James folded his arms about her again, and she sobbed against him. He could not, because of his inherent desire for the casual attitude in emotional crises, tell her at this moment he was ready to die for her. He said, "Idiot . . ." Then she was lost in him and ceased to sob so long as his arms bound her.

≈≈≈

Now again in the cabin, the tears welled and rolled down her cheeks. It wasn't just the separation, but the fact that he turned from her, walking into danger.

The bosun's whistle stabbed her, sounding the immediate out of the past.

Sue's baby stirred, snuffling and beginning to cry. Helen sat up. It was no use trying to sleep.

"I'm going to walk," she whispered to Sue, who, switching on the light and bending over the baby, did not notice Helen. She lifted the baby, rocking it gently in her arms.

Helen heard her whisper solemnly, "*Ssssh*, little Jerry, stop your crying!" Her voice filled with sobs. "Don't you think I'd like to cry? Don't you think I'd rather have your Daddy any day?" And then she kissed him roughly and rocked him, burying her face against him.

The baby yawned, hushed and comforted, as Helen slipped out into the gusty cold of the passageway.

8

EVEN THE SHIP SEEMED TO SENSE DANGER TONIGHT, rocking like a frightened old woman, waiting for the rumbling in her gut to kill her — miserable and creaking in the fog. Only the dimmed cabins and sultry wardroom had lights. The blackout tonight seemed blacker because of the fog, to have condensed into a living mass.

The fog crept in the instant a deck door opened, sweeping down the passageways salt and damp, slicing the swirls of cigarette smoke that floated out of the cabins.

At some of the cabin doors Helen heard singing and the snapping of cards. Helen knew the stakes were high — months of pay — and the games perpetual. She caught the whiff of gin, heard explosions of laughter.

The gaiety couldn't stop itself, didn't dare to

put its ear to the porthole and listen to the sloshing of the inky sea beneath a choking fog.

The ship was cruising, swung back on her wake, the foghorns out of San Francisco left behind. They were heading west again. Some said they would redouble and put in at Los Angeles or even San Diego. Some said they would outdistance the sub.

Helen wondered at the apparent unconcern, the gaiety; perhaps they still could not comprehend their own position in world war; or were they gay because there was nothing else, except hysteria? Helen knew they were different — she was different — from the ignorant trumpeting buffoons she had witnessed the night before the war. Big talk, petty quarrels; suddenly and ludicrously, in the midst of dangers, with the moisture of fog in her throat and the hum of engines in her ears, she remembered guiltily she had never decided on what hors d'oeuvres to serve her guests but that Ahulani — dear God, bless her — had blossomed forth with greater ingenuity than a chef from Trader Vic's.

≈≈≈

Helen had stood in the bay of the bedroom watching James dress. His movements as he adjusted his tie and combed his hair were deliberately careful, the result of long acquaintance with the human body in pain and sickness. He was too careful; she turned nervously to the window.

The wind from the Pali was rustling through the coconut palms, shaking the tattered leaves of the banana plant. The rain had stopped and the steam rose from the earth. From up the valley came the echo of barking dogs, the *baa*-ing of goats, and a last cockcrow. In the mango tree on the terrace the mynah birds harangued from their roosts. Helen loved their nonchalant brass, their fat bodies and their beady insolent eyes accented by a ring of white. She watched them strut about the lawn each morning, self-possessed and caustic.

"Are you dressed, dear?" James had finally adjusted his tie, and was studying the fit of his white dinner jacket. Helen saw his face was faintly bronzed against the cold shadowy depth of the mirror, the bamboo blinds streaked the wall behind his head, his white shirt front gleamed — virginal! she smiled — and the scarlet hook of the lobster-claw blossoms grew stiffly in the earthen pot at his elbow. His elbow — she leaned forward.

"There's a smudge on your elbow, James."

"What? Oh, damn!" He brushed it vigorously,

then turned to admire her. She wore a gown of turquoise silk, carefully draped over her full round breasts and shapely hips. Her bare tanned arms were barbarously weighted with silver, a slash of vermilion lipstick neatly accented her lips, and around her neck she wore a dozen strands of white *pikaki* flowers strung in *leis*. James took her by the shoulders and kissed her forehead. He was proud of her beauty, and happy to parade it.

"*Ummm* — smells good! What is it, 'Ecstasy'? Or 'Passion's Flower' or 'Tonight is —' "

"I hear the cars coming." Helen leaned wearily against the warm solidity of his body, the fabric of his coat rough against her cheek. He ran his hand across the back of her neck, felt the tension in her shoulders.

"Beautiful . . ." James whispered, pressing his fingers into the folds of silk, searching underneath for her young body as Helen's hands sought the back of his head, her finger tips cool, her mouth fused to his. They swayed together, floating buoyantly on the crest of their desire, and yet each new embrace left Helen bitter and tormented. To conceive, to give birth, were creative acts that in their joyous love and agony absolved the soul.

In a torture of reluctance, James divided them.

Lacking words they went into the living room. The brisk chatter of men and women flowed up the garden path. Sleek automobiles nosed down the driveway, crunching the gravel, purring smoothly. Filipino boys in white scurried about the rooms.

Helen refreshed her lipstick as James lit a cigarette and stared with a glassy, determined eye into the bamboo cage of parakeets. Suddenly the yellow male blinked a transparent lid and bobbed upside down on his roost, his tail pointed at the ceiling. The pale blue female squawked raucously, and preened her feathers.

"Fool!" James muttered furiously at the bird.

Helen watched the company shifting about, hot and listless, hunting for a cool corner. The naval officers stood neatly buttoned in their snug whites, the army officers, equally outfitted, threw back their shoulders to keep their clothes from sticking to their backs while the women, lightly dressed, baring their browned bodies and brilliantly decorated with gay silks and linens, looked cool and fresh as flowers. They met and chatted, laughing with casual amicability. They were the lords of the island. They were not friends, but a clan that acted friendly, taking possession of the rooms and lawns, easily, perhaps a little scornfully.

The house stood open to the air. The sick lush beauty of the night was pushed back beyond the circle of lamps that lit the garden. Beyond the light the darkness breathed with a warm cloying breath. The insects crawled, feeding their hard fat bodies on the luxuriant foliage. A brown centipede, big as a man's finger, slept under a coconut, and the rough-skinned *buffa* — imperturbable toad in his poisonous flesh — hopped about rustling dinner.

The musicians struck up the Royal Hawaiian War Dance. From across the valley came the voices of listening natives, singing.

The lazy songs and persistent inane chatter made Helen quiver inwardly. Her legs were aching and would spoil the fun of dancing.

"Stupidity, stupidity!" she chanted to herself as she went smiling among her guests.

"How are you, Jerry? Isn't it a lovely evening? Will you have another drink? No? Nor I!"

"I suppose Kurusu will smooth the situation. . . . Did you meet him when he came through on the Clipper?"

"Yes — charming fellow. . . ."

"But they certainly won't dare to hold out for

concessions in the Netherlands East Indies. . . . Well, I suppose that is the civilian attitude, but we can't let them. Supposing they did get in, would they be satisfied? . . . Good faith? Hell!"

"We've been itching to shoot up those yellow-bellies since, good God, let me think, . . . since they went into Shanghai."

"Oh, before that!"

"I say we ought to put them in their place now. They want to own the Pacific — not just trade, but rule!"

"Six to half-dozen of the other, isn't it?" Jerry murmured laconically, with a cheery grin.

"Not altogether," James answered roughly.

"As I was reminding Sue on the way over here, this is exactly the same talk I heard years ago in Cheefoo. That was long before the China war — so we can't get too worked up over this crisis. War with Japan? Perhaps, someday, we'll steam right up to their fleet and give it to 'em — broadside!" Jerry rubbed his hands together gleefully.

"Uncle Sam will let 'em have it, eh, Jerry?" James spoke soberly, his hands shoved deep in his pockets as he rocked on his heels.

"They say the football team from the mainland is quite . . ." Helen suggested feebly, hoping that

James would change the conversation. He didn't. She knew Jerry had heard, but rejected her gracefully by smiling a "What can I say, Helen?" smile.

"What about the docks here in Honolulu? I understand our ships are lying off port — you can usually see them from this house — badly delayed in unloading. It slows down all the shipping from the mainland. Lord knows, extra docks might lower the premiums on docking privileges, but think of the difference in the quantity of vital materials flowing in! In the long run, the time saved in docking would write off the cost of additional construction."

"James Marin, the man with the long-range attitude!" Jerry laid a friendly hand on James's shoulder.

"But why in hell should we increase the dockage space with present profits as great as they are? Consider the risk if this so-called 'national crisis' blows over. It would mean an outlay of cash that none of us care to consider." John B. Brassfield, red and fiftyish, puffed quickly on his cigar and laughed scornfully. He fixed Jerry with his pale blue eyes. "We aren't in business for our health, you know the old saying — and we don't get goods cut-rate from Uncle Sam like some of you boys. . . . As I told the legislature, if the Navy wants docks, let them build them!"

James grew hot under the collar; Brassfield was hitting too low. "Every time the Navy tries to make a move they confront obstacles — you know that, Brassfield — and I won't name names, but — " but Jerry laid a warning hand on James's arm and prevented a nasty eruption, for Brassfield was not one to have his dealing displayed in any but a favorable light.

"As I was saying," he went on, "let the Navy go ahead. What the Navy does is absolutely no concern of ours! This is an American territory, free, white — all that — damn if I like their meddling in free enterprise — or business of any sort." He spluttered the amendment as James's lips formed the words: "Brassfield Enterprises . . ."

James clapped his hand to his forehead. "What a headache! Tell me, Brassfield, when are the Navy and Territory going to come to some agreement on anything? It seems to me — and free enterprise included — that a small island like this needs the protection of the Navy. Or doesn't it? Look how the Jap Navy took to horning into Hilo Harbor a few years ago, thanks to local free enterprise. . . ."

"The protection, but not the interference . . ."

"But this Navy Base is supposedly for the protection of the mainland. Suppose the Navy did build the docks — they'd be turned over to commercial trade later."

"By God! That's communism!" Brassfield roared, throwing away his cigar.

"What?" James gasped. "That? That's common sense! Is it communism to give them to private industry later? You're waving a red herring under the wrong nose, J. B."

"How do we know the government might not keep them? Besides, James, we don't need the docking space. Those ships out there will be unloaded in a few days. What's a day or two? I'll be damned if we're going to take a financial loss to please a few Annapolis old boys!"

"Then you resent the primary conclusion that this is a military base to protect the mainland?"

"Protect the mainland, hell! Can we help it if the mainland gets the war jitters? We're not playing tiddlywinks. What about the foreign interests here? Ask them — don't you think they're closer to the situation than we? They have men in Singapore. . . . If the Navy wants docks they'll build without our bothering to lift a finger, or lose our shirt because someone yells, 'Wolf!'"

"What do you say to that, Jerry, being Navy?"

Jerry rubbed his hand over his chin, still grinning cheerfully. "Well, James, you know how it is . . ." He shrugged. "Perhaps Admiral Nelson could put his telescope to his blind eye to read his commander's orders, and win the battle of Copenhagen — but not Jerry. I'm a lieutenant — and I like being a lieutenant. . . ." And for the third time he tapped a gentle warning on James's arm.

"What about the bottlenecked Pearl Harbor road?" James turned accusingly on Brassfield. He wasn't afraid of a stomach ulcer that refused to respond to any other doctor on the island. He knew Brassfield's belly inside and out, and it pleased his pride to be able to handle a powerful man like Brassfield. To crack the whip by waving a stomach pump. . . . "What about that road, Brassfield?"

"Let the Navy handle it — it's for their use."

"And the single road to Schofield from Pearl Harbor?"

"That's for the Army!"

Helen felt her arm gripped by a warm, horny paw. "I like your house." Jane, her nails blunt and none too clean, her dress outrageously elaborate, leaned into Helen's face, speaking in a husky voice.

"Thank you, Jane, we enjoy it. It's a wonderful spot to see both Honolulu and Pearl Harbor — but the lease was rather steep for such flimsy construction."

"Don't mention rents! They're awful! But as J.B. said the other day, *we* can't complain. Men have a right to share in defense profits. Don't pay rent myself — although we've been thinking of leasing the house — "

"Leasing your house? The Honolulu house?"

"Oh, it's just a notion. J.B. wanted to go to the mainland on business — "

"Leaving the Islands? You usually wait until spring, Jane. It would be so cold on the mainland."

"I'm not leaving. My boy's here. . . . J.B. just had the notion to go now instead of later. But I'm staying here. Anyway, as I told you, J.B. says we shouldn't criticize where we aren't concerned . . . these defense profits, renting . . ." Jane laughed hoarsely.

Helen recalled that Mr. Brassfield, ten times a millionaire, had very well concerned himself, and quite profitably, with profiteering. There was something James had mentioned about political contracts dovetailing into a lucrative business . . . something about dredging the channels and then sub-dividing the resurrected ocean bottom and selling it for houselots. She said:

"Of course not, Jane, you do enough for people as it is. That recent endowment . . . won't it be interesting, that study of the Polynesian canoe?" Helen smiled blandly.

Jane grunted. "Jack's idea — not mine. Would've spent the money on a home for old dogs, myself."

They were walking across the lawn. Helen's legs cried out for her to rest as she stumbled on the uneven flagstones. "The Polynesians were so adventurous . . ." she said without a spark of interest. Jane ignored her. She never stopped talking about dogs. Helen felt a mosquito sting her cheek, and another her ankle.

". . . And the big one, the spotted one, had distemper all last month. I almost lost him. Now Betty, the one that sleeps on my bed — you've seen her — white, lean, beautiful . . . Helen, d'you suppose James could do something with her? I've had her to every vet on the Islands, and so far . . . He handles J.B. so well, and I know Betty is a lot more responsive . . . Helen, what's the matter?"

"Jane Brassfield!" Helen was in tears. Jane's straw had broken her. "James is not a vet!" All her boredom, all her miserable forced inertia, gave way to one desire: to turn into a whip and lash out hard against these people.

"Well, the more I see of humans the better I — You look sick; in fact, Helen, you look awful!" They were on the steps, then through the door. Inside the house Jane Brassfield strode angrily away.

"What did you say to her?" James whispered. Helen smiled and lifted a finger to her lips.

"Couldn't we just poison our guests, darling?" And she glanced down hurriedly to hide her tears of exhaustion.

"Must you insult them?"

"They've dirtied our house!" She stood still and straight in anger, the hollows under her cheekbones dark with brooding illness, her green eyes half shut.

"Be still! They'll hear you. . . . You're mean, Helen." James gripped her arm. He, too, was suddenly tired. His eyes fixed on her crippled legs. "You're bitter, and it's made you contemptible and little!"

Helen gasped. "Thank you!"

"What do you want out of life? No one is good enough for you!"

"Oh my God, James, can't you understand? Are they so important to you? Must I love them?" A laugh began and ended on Helen's lips, her eyes were in agony. "Perhaps it would help your professional standing! Shall I go to bed with them?"

James began to whisper hoarsely, "I don't know that I'd give a damn — bed with whomever you please!"

Helen smiled a dry, tight smile. "James dear, you're soiling your lovely bedside manner . . ." She felt her body whip taut again, quivering for action. The people in the room became transparent, the minutest subtleties of their chatter rang like bells in her ears. It was a moment of perception so intense it had its own peculiar joy. Helen rose to meet it, but James was spilling over, turning on his temper, his nice dignity running out on the floor.

Helen wanted to ask: Why, James, are you defending this obnoxious flock of cackling Philistines? They are cruel and angry behind their smiles. They've confused you — made you angry — divided your house! The room tilted on one end. Helen leaned in the doorway waiting for the dizziness to pass. There was a leaden weight in her legs. The man beside her who, she recalled, was her husband, was still fuming. . . . He was trying not to see her weakness, trying not to give in again, as always, again and again!

She turned and smiled at him. "Poor James!" Are there no depths or heights for you other than the physical? Are there no jagged cliffs to scale where the air is scant and clean, so close is it to the outer space, to suspension in nothing or in everything, in the Devil or in God? Are there no false steps, my darling, to plunge you weeping into chasms peopled for eternity with Brassfields . . . ? If not — oh, my dear, I pity you! She smiled again, gently, with affection.

"I'm sorry . . ."

James stared at her, then let his eyes follow the line of the door's edge to the floor. "We can't stand here forever."

"No, I'll go see if Ahulani —"

"They'll think we're rude."

"Oh, dear, how horrible! How . . ." She smiled at him again, watching closely how he entered the living room. He seemed somewhat smaller. There had been a pale bewilderment in his gray eyes, and now there was a defiant toss to his right shoulder as he walked slowly away from her.

≈≈≈

Walking alone on the ship Helen longed for James, knowing clearly what their relationship must be: that of love without friendship. She knew now her understanding must make up for the imperfection of the union . . . the fact of her understanding gave grace to her obeisance.

≈≈≈≈

While they were quarreling, the guests had started to dance. The rhythm began in the living room around the bar and expanded into the *lanai*, where the shadows were deep and hid sweet potted plants, out onto the moss in the garden where the Hawaiian musicians were. In and out, in and out, the *leis* the women wore trailed pungent strings of scent and wove invisible patterns among the dancers. The white electric light chalked the faces. The military uniforms gleamed against the pink skin of well-fed bodies.

"Did you hear? We can't go horseback riding at Fort Shafter — the horses, my dear, are off to the wars!" A pretty young army wife turned to Jane.

"Ye Gods! No horses? What'll you Texans do with yourselves?"

"Well, that's the last straw! Thank God, this is my last year here! The tropics — hell!"

"Jerry — no! Doesn't Jerry like the little brown girls — "

"No! No thanks! I'm going in for sheep." Jerry ran his fingers through his hair, frowning.

"Jerry darling, may I be the black sheep in your flock?" This from Beth, the wife of a wealthy grower, whose promiscuous beauty had made her at the early age of thirty-five the creaking dried-up delight of moralists.

"Jerry Marshall, the shepherd boy. Can't you just *see* him! With a long beard — barefooted!" she continued, turning full circle to attract everyone's attention.

"Sue, darlin', you know you'll loathe it," the little army wife from Texas shrilled.

Sue shrugged, her blue eyes tired, her face fixed in a wretched smile. It was their cherished secret, and Jerry had forgotten! Biting back her tears: "I intend to have acres of rolling lawn for — my baby — "

"Baby! On a farm!" Beth screamed. "Oh, my God!"

"Only those nasty draft evaders have babies . . ."

"Who'll mow the rolling lawn, Jerry?"

Unamused, and sorry he'd spoken, Jerry answered grimly, "The sheep."

"Baa baa black sheep!" Beth tittered.

"Helen's had a round with James," Jane interrupted loudly, bored with Beth's humor.

"James needs a drink — to sober him," a Waikiki innkeeper remarked sagely.

"He's very moderate — have you noticed how Helen's limping?"

"Perhaps he beats her . . ." whispered Beth.

"A neat wench — comfortable as — "

"Cut that." Jerry whirled on the innkeeper.

They cheered and wept great tears of laughter into their drinks.

"Sorry." Jerry caught Sue's arm. "Come on, Sue, let's get some air."

Helen found herself dancing with a *haole kamaaina,* a white-haired gentleman who had been a member of the last Queen's household and told nostalgic anecdotes of the corpulent princesses.

"You like Hawaii, Mrs. Marin?" his voice was low and rich, the "a" broad, in the charming languid manner of the islanders.

"It's very beautiful," Helen conceded.

"Oahu has its great possibilities, my dear."

"Yes?" Helen knew he would not be submerged in Chicago or Detroit. There were bigger rackets, but probably no leader more unscrupulous than he.

It was common knowledge that on the side, for nothing more than pin money, he fed women into Brassfield's section near the canal district; they split the profits.

"A fine romantic place." She felt his hand fumbling against her skin, his thumb feeling her breast then moving back quickly to its proper place. She felt his breath pungent on her lips, and nearly gagged.

The dance ended, she went in search of Ahulani. Through the dining-room window she glimpsed Kim, crouched behind the bushes, and waved to him, tossing him a handful of sweets from the nearest bonbon dish.

Ahulani stood in the pantry bossing the caterers, much to their disgust.

"You been dancing too much, Mrs. Marin, let me bring you something." Ahulani paused, crisp in her white apron, her dark hair flaunting a yellow hibiscus. "Don't you go get sick just before Christmas."

Helen nodded. "I'll slip out for a little —" but someone clutched her arm.

"Darling, where's Polly? Must introduce her —"

"Oh, Beth!" Helen whirled nervously. "She's

there — with Jerry." As she turned back to Ahulani, Helen's lips quivered.

"You come sit here, I bring you cup of tea," Ahulani took her hand gently.

"Is anyone in the kitchen?"

"Just those fool catering boys — that's all."

Helen pushed through the swinging door and sank down on a stool. The Filipino boys around the sink and stove bowed politely as Helen smiled and burst into tears.

Using her lean elbows, Beth needled her way through the crowd.

"Polly, Miss Smith of Fresno and Long Beach, California, wants to meet you, a genuine Chinese. She says she never met one — didn't you, Smitty?"

"Not socially, no. . . . But in Rome — this *is* exotic!"

Polly paused in dancing with Jerry, smiling politely, flickers of thoughts behind her eyes. *Not socially*, was it? Dr. Wong, her fiancé, was the best surgeon in the Islands, as well as the son of a wealthy importer. Polly's father had been in the legislature. The Lings and the Wongs could excusably ignore whom they pleased.

"How do you do?" Polly chose to be polite, as she searched anxiously for Dr. Wong in the crowd.

He was turned from her, talking with a Japanese banker, the sponsor of a Japanese language school.

"Oh! Hel-lo — Beth, your island ways are so-o democratic!" Miss Smith fleetingly acknowledged the introduction. "This brushing elbows . . . It just screams Sax Rohmer . . ."

Jerry felt Polly stiffening, and danced her hastily away. He snorted, steering her toward the buffet. "Did you get the locality, Pol? She might have said Bronx and Coney Island. . . . We're not all like that!"

Polly shrugged, laughing. "You're not, anyway, Jerry! Thanks. She's like lots of mainlanders, isn't she?"

"The mainland's big, Pol; some places are slimy with race prejudice, others are like the Islands — where people know their friends."

It took two cups of Ahulani's best tea, sipped to her gentle consoling laughter, to give Helen the courage to wander back into a group of older women who sat on the living-room couch gossiping over their drinks.

"Helen, what are you doing tomorrow?" A question without a particular motive.

"We had thought about the beach. Jackie and Dr. Marin look forward to it every week end."

"Will you go to Lanakai?" — asked without curiosity — "Or the Yacht Club?"

"Possibly — for a dip. But I," Helen began to laugh, knowing how unconcerned they all were with what she said, "I prefer Kahuku. I have a passion for hunting the glass balls."

"Really? What are they good for? I never found one."

"In all these years?" Helen stared at the wife of the *haole kamaaina*. Although her maiden name had come to the Islands with one of the first missionaries, her vigorous determination had been focused for sixty years on bird sanctuaries, Republican meetings, and anti-Catholicism.

Helen posed her question differently: "Don't you like things Japanese?"

"Oh, yes — the Japanese — but they aren't Catholic. My dear, are you a Catholic?"

"No, nor Japanese. . . . I just like glass balls," Helen answered idiotically as she stared at the older woman.

Helen wanted to ask her if she had ever looked along the fierce coast of Kahuku, where the lava thrust a brutal jagged face toward heaven, where the torn seas returned again and again wearing away the inhospitable shore. In all these sixty years, had she never looked into the faces of the little people, the thin consumptive Orientals, overworked Portuguese, the defiant half-breeds? But Jerry touched her elbow and Helen was swept off among the dancers.

The tiny island lying against the ocean's breast sighed and exhaled its sick sweet breath, cradling its warmth in the warm waters. The night air did not chill, but continued hot. One by one, the brilliant holiday lights winked out, until Honolulu dozed against the hills, marked only by the threads of light along its streets and waterfront.

A faint breeze stirred. Helen thought she heard Jacqueline call in her sleep. Finally, even the pugnacious mynah birds were quiet in the mango. The last car rolled down the gravel.

Helen had gone in to James ready to beg forgiveness and have his love. He lay heavily, his face hidden under his arm. When she called his name he would not answer. She knew he was not asleep. Then had Helen bitterly desired him.

≈≈≈

Helen leaned wearily against the corridor walls recalling the dead past. Now tonight, surrounded by the same ocean, borne on a confiscated German ship, moving back — west — circling slowly while hunting for a break in the fog where speed could outrun a submarine, were the same people. Helen pushed back her hair, and, straightening her shoulders, started to walk. That night there had been no foreboding, but tonight . . . She took a deep breath and turned down another passageway.

Behind Helen as she wandered through the ship stalked a restless shadow that paused when she paused and hid when she turned. Since the morning on the hatch, Jeff had lusted after her, angrily, fearful that his broken body was not subservient to his will. He was baffled by these impulses that had never been permitted any physical outlet. He saw his whole life lying smashed before him. He lived in horror for fear that what had never begun was finished. He wondered if sexual impotence would show on his face like a revolting sore.

The cold wind from the ocean brushed his scarred temple and chilled the tissues of the scars underneath his clothes. The hell of a wound was its incessant sensitivity, the shocked nerves helplessly crying. Jeff watched Helen's movement down the passageway, quick, rhythmic. At first glance it had seemed jaunty, but now he recognized the lope of a wounded animal. . . . An officer swung out of a lighted cabin and brushed Jeff against her.

"Beg pardon, sir —"

"I'm sorry, sir — sorry, madam."

Helen spun around. "Hello, Jeff." She held out her hand, "You haven't been ill, have you?"

He shook his head. They stood together, his hand in hers, as the officer passed out of sight. The cabin door swung ajar, permitting a faint light to beam through illicitly. Their faces grew taut with their deeply personal needs. Jeff's bewildered, frightened, withal defiant, and Helen's tired, very lonely, wanting to be free of herself. He put his arms around her. She did not stir but spoke softly.

"It's not I you want — you're seeking me, but you don't need me. It's something else. I'll help you find it. . . ."

"How?"

"I've been through every step you're taking, Jeff, through every agony."

"No! You can't have — you don't know —"

"Are you in love, Jeff?"

He shook his head. "I told you I was once, but now — I don't know — I've got to know!" He couldn't believe his own voice was saying these secret things.

Helen put her hands on his shoulders and

pushed him gently back in order to see his face. His thin mouth turned down, and his eyes were trying to hide his shame. The cabin door slammed shut, closing off the light. The dark hid her face from him as his arms groped for her.

The cold fog intensified the warmth of their hands as they clung together. Cautiously Jeff led her down the passageway, pushed back his cabin door and drew her inside. There was no light, for the porthole was open. The dashing of waves against the ship roared in upon them.

As they stumbled against the bunk they fell to their knees and did not get up. Jeff's arms clasped her, her breasts soft against his, her hips hard against him, her arms were clinging to the bunk above their heads, her body sagging under the weight of his. Her breath was warm against his cheek, her forehead plunged against his shoulder. His insignia cut grooves in her skin and her hair clung to his ear. The darkness wound about them with the wind, and the roar of the waves beneath the plunging ship.

When at last her arms hung limp at her sides she raised her head, "I must go back." He helped her to rise.

Together they groped for the door. "Good night."

With both hands Helen brushed back her hair and breathed the cold salt air. Jeff watched the rise of her breasts and the faint glimmer of light on her wrists. He stood straight, and very still. His voice echoed the security of his mind.

"Good night."

As his door closed Helen leaned for an instant against the ship's wall. She was listening to the creak of the hull, strong and supple like a giant tree in the wind, lifting up and plunging down, the twisting sudden sliding shift to port, to starboard, marking the cautious wake.

A door flew open, a ragged family spilled out and were hurled against the farther wall. In the faint light from the cabin Helen saw Mrs. Sparrow shove herself away from the ship's sides, balancing awkwardly. Her babes rolled and bawled against her cautiously straddled legs.

Helen gave them a friendly nod. "You'd better get some sleep, Mrs. Sparrow. No doubt we'll dock tomorrow."

Mrs. Sparrow stared through eyes clouded with the immediate trouble of keeping her balance. She envied Helen, slender and tall, like waving sea grass, with only her finger tips adjusting her balance against the corridor handrail. But then, Mrs. Sparrow concluded, that Mrs. Marin was something beyond all understanding — as if nothing could hurt her. Mrs. Sparrow shuddered and edged away, a subconscious jealousy reminded her how there in the fog she'd seen Mrs. Marin flirting with God's own minister! Mrs. Sparrow decided that Helen Marin was a bad woman.

"I ain't agoin' to be abed tonight, I ain't. . . . I'll be a prayin' on my knees . . ." she cried out angrily, clutching her children to her.

Helen pressed her hand. "Yes, and so will I, Mrs. Sparrow . . . so will I."

9

The morning world was gray, confined to the gray space between the bow and the stern, the width of the slanting deck and the depth measuring but halfway down the side of the ship to the sluggish gray water below. The dimensions of a crab's world. The ship horn groaned and was answered from all sides. Intense sounds to the ears of the listening blind.

Visibility: zero. The ships lumbered stupidly through the mists, wallowing and moaning. Out of the layers of fog a small boat appeared, chugging softly, a phantom tug only half discerned in the gray wash of slate-colored sea. It lurched sharply to port with a sad little toot, nosing its cautious way around the transport, and was swallowed into the fog once more.

Rumors skulked from wardroom to galley to sick

bay, and up into the crowded civilian and officers' cabins. Tiny children, bored little demons, ran screaming through the passageways. The mothers sat silent, sometimes exchanging stories of horror, picking the civilized red lacquer from their fingernails. Silently they stripped their claws. None wept. Some laughed. They seemed not to care what happened to themselves but they glanced anxiously at the children. Some of the women had already died in spirit in Java and Borneo and China, in Hong Kong, Manila, and Singapore. They had become automatons with a duty in the eyes of society to the children of their vanished lives.

They represented part of a glib phrase, the inflammable catchwords: *Remember Pearl Harbor.* But it was not something to boast or yarn about. A bitter revelation to American egos was human indifference. They learned to cling to inanimate objects: to the ship, to precious steel and ammunition. Numb little barnacles, swung suddenly to the nether pole of human faith, discovering the true meaning of rugged individualism in isolation.

Helen leaned against the rail, watching their cruiser escort shuffling in and out of vision, heard it cry and call to its charges. Suddenly a woman sobbed:

"I hopes to God they don't find us!"

People moved away, uncomfortable for the little scrawny creature, but Helen bent down. "Really, Mrs. Sparrow, nothing will happen. Do you think we want to lose this fine big ship to the Japs? Mrs. Sparrow, you're going to be all right."

Depth charges . . .

"Thank God! Give 'em hell!"

"If it happens — it happens. Look at that movie star killed in a plane right in the States . . ." A pale girl kept her darting eyes on the children playing hide-and-seek around the casks of water and inflated life rafts. "It's sure quiet now."

Helen shivered involuntarily.

≈≈≈

It had been quiet, too, that morning months ago as the Pali mists gathered and a light rain fell upon the ferns and ginger and elephant-ears in the valleys above the town. The Marin party had lasted late. There had been no sudden warning, to their heavy-headed guests, of another day approaching — only a subtle wilting of the rich carnation and *pikaki leis*, a deeper shadow under a youthful eye, a yawn behind a pale hand.

Wearily, Helen had listened to James and Mr. Brassfield droning again.

"Can you give me a financially unprejudiced reason why the Territory and the Military should always be at loggerheads?"

"Good God, James, why should *you* worry about it? How could I divorce profits and loss; it isn't sound. . . . Give us time, man, time — we'll iron it out . . ."

"I think the time is lost."

"Rome wasn't built in a day . . ."

"Neither was Japan," James snapped.

"Say, you've been listening to the alarmists. . . . We ought to have you on our Civilian Defense Committee, put a badge on your arm and let you blow a whistle. . . ."

≈≈≈

The ship's engines vibrated silently beneath the decks. Suddenly the cruiser escort loomed out of the fog off the starboard bow.

"Jesus! We'll crash!"

A warning shell from the transport sent the cruiser back. Helen leaned on one elbow, her chin in her hand, watching as if she were alone on the ship. Then as she swung her mind back into focus she patted Mrs. Sparrow's trembling shoulder, automatically started the frantic children on a charade, assisted the harried Chaplain in his thankless task of trying to cheer the company.

A pain in her hip sharpened, nagging her steps. The fog, no doubt, and her sleeplessness. She had been walking too much. Angrily, she ignored the pain. Her words flowed from her so smoothly she wondered that people did not think them false. "No danger . . . nearly in port . . . nothing to fear . . ." She had to admire the tone of her voice, marveling that anyone listened.

Then it came. The ship, plunging forward, swung crazily about. The passengers stared at each other. An elderly woman, adjusting the pin in her hat, coughed nervously.

≋

No one had remembered afterwards at what moment he had become actually aware of an end of peace and a beginning of war. It was like a new star appearing in the morning sky, at first hardly noticeable in the sunrise, not more than a pin prick. The winds blew gently still, and although the sky was heavy laden with white billowing clouds, the sun shone. . . . And the faint new star was nothing more than a glancing light on the distant waves until the nearness of it began to distort the day. And in its speed, whirling toward them, it became another, greater sun, fierce and hot and thundering as it pushed aside the outer air and bent down on Oahu. It screamed out of the sky into their dew-flecked gardens, tore the earth and threw it high . . . yet, not even then . . . did they fully understand that it had come to blot out forever their accustomed days . . . nor why.

It came with fearful silences when the leaves of the trees hung motionless, it came painted on the wings of Zero planes, in shattering blows of bombs and the hysterical cracking anger of the pitifully inadequate antiaircraft. It splintered arms and legs, it bit off ears and blinded frightened eyes.

It stole down a quiet road where a scarlet cardinal still sang among the rustling palm leaves, and it struck Ahulani Ferrara in the back of the neck. A quick paralyzing blow from behind. Amidst the virile green of towering hills, a brown Hawaiian woman crumpled on a dusty road, a fresh hibiscus glued with blood to her tangled hair.

On a near-by bridge an American-Japanese soldier poured all his rifle bullets into the sky after the plane, sobbing for more bullets to avenge her.

War came suddenly to all the island, like a light turned into the face of a sleeper. It came screeching into Helen Marin's garden.

Helen stood in a silk dressing gown on the *lanai*, her thin hands clasped tight in front of her as she paused beside a bowl of darting, glinting fish. The morning sun streaked her neck with golden bars where it slipped between the thin slats of the bamboo blind. Her curling hair leaped in wild ringlets, tossed back from her forehead. Her lips still tingled where they had pressed against James's. His unshaven cheek had scratched her, and her shoulders were still white with his finger marks. He had been gone an eternity.

The screen door of the *lanai* had swung shut, the winding path lay empty again, even where his feet had run there were no marks, the overhanging branches had ceased to sway where he had pushed a straggler aside. The garage door creaked open. There had been time for him to start the car, and when she thought about it . . . inserting the key in the ignition, the act of turning the switch, the starter down and up again, the mysterious combustion that went on with gasoline . . . Time strode with War, alive, expanding and contracting. Time was a tremendous choral. It ticked busily inside her diamond wrist watch and in the mechanism of a torpedo.

Helen touched her lips. They still tingled from his kiss, the vibration fading slowly, like a note sustained in music, singing clearly even as other notes were struck.

When James had caught Helen by the shoulder, Ahulani had plucked a pale pink hibiscus and stuck it in her hair. While James held Helen tight, Ahulani paused to listen to the cardinal's song and heard instead the roaring of an airplane. At the moment James kissed Helen, Ahulani saw a white light, greater even than the eruption of Mauna Loa when she was a child. When James let Helen go, Ahulani lay still. As the screen door slammed, Ahulani died, a destroyer blew to bits, an airplane dove into the sea beyond Kahuku, a child fell dead on a green lawn, his hands still smelling fresh of soap and toothpaste.

And Kim stood still in the garden, his fists clenching the brown wood roses he had gathered early for Jacqueline. He stared into the sky. There droned the enemy above the blanket of soft clouds. His people: his mother, his father . . .

Jerry and Sue slept heavily, weary of last night. The sheet had been kicked from the bed and, in the warmth of the morning, they lay listening drowsily. Sue heard the sounds of war and stirred, rising on one elbow. The sunlight pricked her eyes, somewhere she smelled coffee and bacon and eggs being cooked. She rested her chin on Jerry's shoulder and whispered:

"Jerry."

"*Ummm?*"

"Are they having target practice today, Sunday?"

"*Ummm.* Must be." Jerry drew his shoulder away, for the contact with her skin left a warm sticky patch on him. He flopped on his stomach and put the pillow over his head. The telephone jangled him out from under the cool linen.

"Gosh. Who in . . ." He stretched a naked arm above his head, and Sue saw the sun turn the hairs to bronze on a bronze arm. His wrist watch glowed in the sun, a white light swelling, oscillating as the beam met the curve of the dial; then all of it dropped into shadow.

"Hello. . . . Who? Who? Say, who do you think you are? Go back to bed and sleep it off!"

"This is no God-damn joke, Lieutenant!"

"The hell!" Jerry hung the telephone on its rack and gripped Sue in his arms. His eyes snapped suddenly, his breath was short. "Here it is, old girl, right in our own back yard!"

Sue drank her coffee on the *lanai,* her eyes glued to the sleek new roadster snorting down the road. Out of the sky she thought she saw a dark bird flying. . . . The sun burst on the back of Jerry's roadster. The sun? "My God! No, Jerry, no! My God!"

There was a monkey-pod tree in the center of the Lings' garden and a stream gurgling past. The ginger blossoms dipped into the waters, trembling, causing faint merry ripples with every reverberation of the guns. Polly clung to her brother Isaac's hand. "Do you remember, Isaac, when we were little, no? Our father telling us of the Japanese?" Her voice was so low that Isaac had to strain to hear, but even as he listened he told himself the day was different. A special day to be carefully observed. Not merely Sunday, but Sunday, December seventh, one thousand nine hundred and forty-one. He imagined other children, now unborn, writing it laboriously on a sheet of foolscap in answer to a history question! It was a beautiful day, hot moist, the sky hung with garlands of clouds. Were they thrown over to protect the land, like the gray fog at Dunkirk? Isaac clenched his fists. Didn't the great Christian God know how high those Japs could fly and how sickening it was to watch the black blobs of smoke from the antiaircraft bursting a thousand feet short of the target?

"Those dirty Japs!" Isaac shuddered.

They sat side by side on the moss and Polly, her thin fingers shaking and cold, began to weave a *lei* of flowers. Isaac watched her with mingled scorn and fascination. With each concussion the earth shook beneath them, overhead the constant bark of the helpless antiaircraft and mere machine guns mounted on trucks, and the drone of planes made them turn to jelly in their stomachs, but there they sat, two graceful Oriental figures, pale, speaking softly, twining flowers.

Polly and Isaac heard the whining whistle dropping toward them. Polly stopped, listened, her face a hard ivory mask. Suddenly Isaac caught her in his arms. He lay upon her in the grass, pressing his body the length of hers, a low choking noise bubbling foolishly between his teeth. A clod of dirt struck him beneath the eye, spreading brown dust across their faces. Isaac's ears plugged with the concussion of the bomb. He looked at Polly, her lips parted, moving silently.

She was praying to her gods. The white man's way with his single god and multiple devilish machines had betrayed them. She prayed to darkly curling shadows behind silent flames.

Helen Marin prayed, too. She had no consciousness of passing time. But time was passing. The tingle on her lips had vanished. The pressure on her shoulders faded. Slowly she sank down on the hard mat, her silken dressing gown billowing around her knees. She watched as the round fish bowl caught the light in flaming pulsations, the shooting rays prismatic, splendid. A tiny coral lizard, no bigger than a cricket, paused a moment pierced by the javelins of light, then scurried down the screen and snapped a yellow spotted fly.

Helen folded her hands and stared down on the city. This is it. This is war. Those bursts of white and scarlet are bombs! Look there — and there — and over there! Look up and down and out to sea. Look hard on death.

I am Helen Marin. I am white. I am an American. I am a citizen of the United States. . . . Tell me, please, where is the nearest consulate?

But this *is* the United States!

Her lips parted as she continued to stare. Sparks of memories flashed in her mind, then ignited in one flame of realization. She felt a momentary panic and immediately thought of James. Where was he? Where? Working, too busy sweating (how he hated the tropics when he had surgery), certainly he had no time to stare through a fish bowl wondering at a battle.

"Dear God, take care of James . . ." What else did one say? What does one do? In Europe they have shelters, they have a duty to perform, wardens, but here . . . "Dear God, take care of James . . ." Something screamed through the air above the house and crashed far up the valley. Shells? They came speeding horizontal to the earth. Where were they coming from? From enemy ships beyond the horizon? Or from our own guns, from the smoking flashes of our own ships lying in the harbor, carelessly turned on our own people?

She pressed her eyeballs with her palms until bright painful colors sprang under her lids and swirled enchantingly. Behind her she heard Jacqueline stumbling through the house, calling her. "Dear God, spare James! Spare him!" It had been years since she had prayed. Jacqueline stood behind her in the doorway.

"Mother . . ." Jacqueline's face wrinkled like a sheet of burning paper. "Mamma!"

"The Japs . . . It's an air raid, Jackie," Helen answered softly. The words had a touch of the fantastic. "War, darling . . . Well, we're in the war. . . . Jackie, don't cry! We're Americans! There are millions on the mainland. . . ."

They knelt together on the *lanai*, watching. Below them lay the Pacific, gray-blue, unruffled. A ship appeared that had slipped through the harbor bottleneck. They identified a lone United States destroyer. Helen's fingers tightened on Jacqueline's shoulders. A Japanese plane zoomed behind the ship, like a furious bee. The ship darted frantically to port, to starboard, to port again, leaving a crooked wake. Behind her, so close her decks were drenched, bombs exploded in the sea. Geysers of white foam shot up silently, because the din on shore was constant.

Helen's eyes smarted from staring so long at one spot. Then, without warning, the plane lifted its fury into the muffling clouds, and disappeared. The destroyer veered again to starboard and slackened speed. Jacqueline's mouth dropped open, her eyes fixed on the water. She chuckled abruptly, childishly.

In a hastily rigged operating room at Pearl Harbor, Dr. Marin shook his head. Swiftly the nurses removed a little Japanese workman and placed a white-faced ensign on the operating table. His foot was neatly picked of flesh. The bone lay bare.

"Easy now," James murmured. "Steady." The young man moaned. He pressed his lips together fainting.

"They have a blood bank under way at Queen's . . ."

"Thank God!"

"Ever heard of the 'golden hours,' sonny? That's the time we have to patch you up before any infection sets in."

A trembling Filipino boy stared fixedly at James, his mouth screwed in a plaintive pucker, his right hip blown away.

"It will hardly matter to him."

"I wish to hell they'd quit shaking this shack with their God-damn bombs!"

"Where's your wife, doctor?"

"Home — I guess," James bent closer to his patient.

Kim stood with his thin arms pressed against his sides, his head thrown back, staring into the sky between the swishing palm leaves and the sharp angle of the broad eaves. His fingers, aching and sweating, were still clamped around the crumbling brittle wood roses. Slowly he raised his hand to his eyes and opened his fingers. The cracking seed pods were broken, their dry petals chipped, the black seeds dropping on the ground. He let them go. He heard Mrs. Marin call from the *lanai*.

"Kim, where is your mother? Kim!"

Kim shook his head. "I don't know. I haven't seen her, Mrs. Marin, not since this . . ." His voice failed him, something inside him swelled and swelled. He looked back at Mrs. Marin, and beside her, at Jacqueline. Her golden hair hung about her shoulders, her heart-shaped face was cold, drawn, frightened. "I don't know where Ahulani is." Where am I? I am Japanese. Kim's face was quivering, his mouth, his eyes, even his thin arching nostrils quivered. He felt the jerk of muscles in his eyeballs as he tried to open his eyelids wide, holding the lids steady. Otherwise he would cry.

He fixed his gaze on a low hanging cloud and wondered how long it would be before he began to vomit.

The surge and pounding in his head beat so loudly he no longer heard the screeching shells and whining drone of planes. He didn't hear the warning whistle falling out of the sky. He saw nothing but a blue void and one scarlet cardinal wheeling. Something struck him cruelly across the shoulder, for a moment he thought it was a coconut, and then a certain lightness in his legs, the air rushing past his face, made him believe that he was flying through space behind the cardinal. The ground heaved at him and a root struck his temple. He put out his hand and pushed it away. He would not lose sight of the cardinal! I must not lose him! And he began to sob. Suddenly his stomach writhed. He felt everything inside him pull loose and pour out on the ground. He must hurry now, for the cardinal was almost out of sight. He thought he heard Jacqueline cry out, and although the voice was cruel he tried to rise and go to her. "Oh, Mother! Mother Ahulani . . ." and he writhed sick with agony.

Helen raised her head and stared. The earth ceased shaking and the floor beneath them held.

Behind her, through the house, she saw the sky. Slowly she got up from her knees and took a tottering step forward, her arms outstretched. She took another inquiring step. Jacqueline was beside her, her hand in Helen's, her breath whistling in and out between her drooping lips.

"Kim . . ." Helen plunged through the house, scrambling over the ruined walls, and knelt beside the screaming boy. "Jacqueline! Jacqueline! For God's sake call a doctor . . . call James . . . call anyone! Hurry!" She did not see Jacqueline standing white and silent in the ruins of her bedroom.

"This is my house! My house!"

"Jackie!" Helen stared in wonder at the child.

Slowly Jacqueline's face burned scarlet. She dug her fists into her mouth. "No! I won't! I won't!" The joyful secrets of the night before sickened her, she gasped for breath, sobbing, "Kim!" she screamed, "Kim, you dirty Japanese!" She ran like a frightened animal, back through the house, bewildered, utterly betrayed.

Out Diamond Head way, "Waikiki of town," Mr. Brassfield kicked the shattered fragments of a vase under a chair and stared thoughtfully out of the window. Not that he'd ever liked the damned vase anyway, but it had been his property and he certainly intended to file a complaint with the Navy for shooting those big guns without warning. Behind him the telephone was ringing wildly. Finally, realizing that no servant was coming to answer it, he answered it himself.

"J. B. Brassfield speak — "

"Ensign Brassfield, this . . ."

"Wait-a-minute!" J. B. Brassfield tossed the phone on the table. "Jack! Oh, Jack!" He shouted through the window at his wife and son. "Phone."

Jack Brassfield looked up, a lean ruddy boy like a mirror-distorted version of his stout and ruddy mother. He put down his cup of coffee, picked up his cigarette, and strode across the lawn, stopping for a moment to pat his hounds.

The French doors of the living room opened out upon a brick terrace. The floor of the house was brick overlaid with grass mats and gaudy Chinese rugs. The room was furnished lavishly with golden Buddhas, teakwood chests and tables. There were several out-size silver cups, hunting trophies, and innumerable stony-eyed fish mounted on planks.

John picked up the phone. "Hal-lo." He stared vacantly out of the window, watching the puffs of smoke from the big guns on Diamond Head. Some of those crazy fliers were going to get shot down if they weren't more careful!

"Ensign Brassfield . . . This is no God-damn joke. . . . We're under attack! Report to your ship. . . . I said, this is no God-damn joke — it's war!" The receiver clicked in Jack's ear. He replaced the telephone on its red lacquer base — red to look Chinese — and scowled.

"Oh, Dad, will you tell Mother that I can't take her over to the Lanakai house?"

"Why not?"

"Some damn maneuvers going on. . . . I'll shave and dress."

"Jack!" Jane Brassfield bellowed from the terrace. "Where in hell are the servants? Where are Atsuko and Watanabe?"

Mr. Brassfield walked to the door and rang the bell. No answer. He hurried out into the kitchen. No servants.

"They've gone! Probably scared out of their fool wits by all this nonsense."

"Well, you would hire Japs," from Jack.

"And why not?"

"Yeah. Yeah. I know — I know. Well, I'm going up to shave, and if that guy calls again tell him I'm on my way."

J. B. Brassfield had returned to the window. He stared out to sea for some time; finally he asked his wife, poking his head through the door, "You know how much it costs to fire a big gun like that?"

The emergency rescue crew found Mr. Huan, the curio dealer, dead in his shop, lying in blood that glistened with priceless bits of jade and milky ivory. He had fallen in front of a heavily carved chest. His desk had vomited its contents on the floor. Among immaculate envelopes and carefully filled ledgers, a small clay bank for China Relief had bruised his face and spread gray chalk across his cheeks.

The local radio stations cut out their regular commercials and Sunday symphonies and sermons, and began to bark out orders to the people. Workers, soldiers, sailors — report to the Naval Base; and doctors — all doctors — report immediately to Tripler.

Dr. Wong, Polly's fiancé, pressed the accelerator to the floor as he swung on the Kamehameha Highway and then slammed on the brakes. The roadway was a squirming mass of automobiles. He groaned.

He had time to remember a conference in St. Petersburg in 1904 with Japanese delegates who knew that this time guns backed their diplomacy ... and the Russian fleet at Port Arthur sunk without warning! And now again. Here was the Jap. It had happened in Korea and in China, too; but Wong knew that was only Russia, and only China and Korea — while this was America! Was it not sometimes wise to listen to the accumulated wisdom of one's ancestors?

He glanced at his wrist watch — 9:30! He tried his horn. Perhaps he could bluff his way through the jam. Men were dying and he was stuck behind a vegetable truck. He tried to pass, but a Model T swung out in front of him and blocked his move. Dr. Wong beat his horn with his fist. Where were the traffic officers?

Other cars were lined behind him, honking frantically. Here and there were automobiles strafed, bloody, gutted, nosed in the ditch or left squarely in the way. The trucks in front of Dr. Wong were barely moving. Fury blinded Wong. Sitting at the wheel of one truck was an old college chum.

Wong shouted at him, "Hey, you, Matsuda, get out of my way!"

The man looked up, smiled, slowly shaking his head. "Whats-hellsa-matta wit you, Wong? I gotta get through, too."

Wong felt the perspiration pouring down his face. Once they had been friends, educated; now: a wall of blood between them.

≋

10

A WALL OF BLOOD . . .

Helen stared into the fog. Out there was the Jap again. There was a choked triumphant yell: "They've missed us!" as the ship roughed an angular wake. The cruiser darted across their bow and depth-charges rumbled.

The fog flowed in, between the railing and the cabins. It was impossible to see what had happened. Voices began to surmise, elaborate and vouch. Helen gripped Jacqueline's trembling shoulder and pushed her back into the angle of the companionway. They felt the ship gaining speed. Twenty knots — twenty-five — back and forth she jarred against the swells.

Mrs. Sparrow sobbed, her mouth wide, her voice lost. The women picked their nail polish and screamed unheeded commands at their children.

Their faces were scarlet, the veins swollen on their temples. The children, mouths hanging, eyes staring, adult lines of anguish on their smooth young faces . . .

Jacqueline opened her mouth, tears burned her eyes. Helen smiled and Jacqueline's stomach contracted into a fist clenched in her middle.

"Mother . . ." Helen's fingers squeezed Jackie's shoulders steadily, bravely. Jackie clung to Helen, afraid she would vanish, and Helen's fingers, holding Jackie, held all of her life that was real.

The harder Jacqueline buried her face in the soft curve of Helen's neck the more senseless the world became. The tighter she shut her eyes the clearer she saw one image. She sobbed hysterically in Helen's arms and all the while her brain focused on one boy, walking gingerly down a long flight of stairs as he left the hospital with Helen.

≈≈≈

"The air — is good — " Kim tried to grin. "Hi, Jackie!" his smile twisted awkwardly.

"Hi, Kim." Jackie had the car door open for him. "Sit back — way back. . . . How d'you feel?" Her eyes were round with compassion.

"S-swell . . ."

"Kim's fine." Helen had patted his shoulder reassuredly and crawled behind the steering wheel. "Where are the keys?" She climbed out of the car and searched the pockets of her uniform. "I wonder if James took them. Wait here." And she disappeared back into the hospital. In the cool disinfected hall James said:

"I'm going on a call, I'll drop him on the way."

"James, are you sure Joe Ferrara wants him? I thought I'd go in with him . . ." Helen's eyes met the hardness of his and flinched. "Couldn't we . . ." she swallowed the rest of it, afraid of arousing James. He was overworked and angered easily. Twice he had snapped at her about her interest in Kim, and once she had seen him start to remove the bandages roughly only to pause, and, calling a nurse, caution her to do it gently.

"Are you asking to *adopt* him? For God's sake, Helen, he's a Jap — a little Jap bastard — "

"Oh, don't. How can you?"

"I pulled him through, didn't I? Well, didn't I?" He waited until Helen nodded. "I gave him all of my skill — didn't I?"

"Yes."

"Then let me handle it!"

Helen went back to the car, her legs dragging painfully.

"James will drive you in a few minutes. He has

a call. . . ." She tried not to see the peculiar strain that crept into Kim's face. She took some change from her pocket. "Jackie, run get Kim some oranges while you're waiting. The juice is good for you, Kim." She patted his shoulder again.

Jackie had bought two dozen. They were expensive and James looked cross when he saw them.

"Kim will need all of the back seat, Jackie. Sit up front!"

They didn't talk. James stamped the brake hard for the curves and jerked the car up old Booth Road. The Joe Ferrara house was about two hundred feet beyond the bridge where the paving ended in a path.

"Can you make it to the house from here, Kim?" James reached back and opened the rear door without getting out of the car.

"S-sure — thanks, Dr. Marin." Kim didn't look at him but struggled out of the car, clutching the bag of oranges in his left hand. As he walked away, Jackie gasped.

"Wait, Kim, I'll help you!" Kim paused, his head cocked on one side, but James held Jacqueline's elbow.

"Good-by, Kim," he waved. "Be careful of that arm."

Kim nodded. His jaw worked bravely and finally produced a smile.

"Let me go!" Jacqueline hissed, trying to pull her father's fingers off her elbow. "He's hurt . . . let me go!" She began to scream.

"Shut up!" James slammed the car into reverse, spun it around and lurched back down the road scattering goats and chickens and narrowly missing a party of Orientals on foot.

"But Mother said to help him!" Jacqueline sobbed.

"And didn't I?" James voice was cold, level, threatening as a knife blade.

"Yes, but — "

"Then drop it, Jacqueline. . . . Kim has his home. His family. Let him go there." James's face was suddenly pale and tired as Jacqueline tried in vain to read the meaning of his words.

"I guess you did *save* his life," she said weakly.

James had not answered her.

A wall of blood. With every battle Helen saw the wall rise higher like a tidal wave and saw no way to stop it. Up and up it swelled at her.

As the races of man were divided, within the races nations sought chimera supremacy, city fought city, man fought man. It was not only man's racial but man's human problem. Helen marveled that anyone rode the wave. She saw the infinite complexities as a seething mass of colorless good and ill will that perhaps merged in some ultimate reality beyond birth and death. Even in the teeth of personal defeats, personal losses, Helen sought to maintain this recognition.

"Have you ever lived in China, Polly?" Helen had asked her as they sat planning the last details of the Marins' party.

"Yes, for a year or two in Shanghai — and as a child I lived for a while in Calcutta — I wasn't comfortable there." Polly twisted her engagement ring thoughtfully. She was dressed smartly in a colorful play-frock. She had discarded her thick-soled imported sandals in the morning heat and was pattering about barefooted, as was Helen. She had taken over the arrangement of the flowers for that evening. She had the Oriental's tasteful discrimination combined with the Occidental's will to see a task quickly and efficiently accomplished.

"Do you prefer it here?"

"Naturally. This is my home," Polly's tone refused to be serious as she bent to improve the curve of a fern.

"A very practical reason. Aren't there any others?" Helen had curled in a rattan chair.

"I am an American of Chinese parentage. I have two thoughts: Oriental — Occidental. One is the way of my ancestors, the other the way of the white man. In our hearts we follow the way of our forefathers and in our obvious physical acts we follow the white man. Our minds learn to act in two ways, split. . . ."

Helen shrank into her chair. "Two?" Dancing — walking . . . The friends of love — the friends of business?

Polly darted her a look of wonder, but with a nervous smile nodded and laughed, "Yes." She let it fall ambiguously.

Two thoughts — two answers. Helen knew the white man's way. What was the way of the Oriental? Helen was not sure. Was James right? Was it better, perhaps, not to try to understand them, when they were apparently so willing to come across the gap themselves, and skillfully follow your own patterns? Still, there were two patterns! Helen was vaguely uneasy.

She took a cigarette and struck a match to light

it. The sun streamed through the bamboo blinds and for an instant met the flame. She watched the fire vanish in the greater light. Then, below the match, slanting across the coffee table, she saw the silent curling shadow of the flame!

"Ahulani!" she had shouted, blowing out the match. The disconcerting shadow vanished, too.

There was a slow shuffle through the house, of grass sandals on grass mats. Utterly without premonition of approaching death, Ahulani entered convoyed by her tumbling, dark-eyed babes. Her hands were covered with flour. There was flour on the backsides of four or more of the impudent youngsters. In Ahulani's dark and tangled hair was the inevitable hibiscus. She grinned at Helen.

"Will you bring us iced tea please, Ahulani? This weather's awful." Then to Polly, "Wouldn't it be fun if we went naked!"

Helen had stalked restlessly to the screen door of the *lanai*. In the back of her mind a shadow curled and writhed. Was there no answer for the living? She brushed back her hair, feeling feverish.

Day and night the climate was the same. Even in the downpour of afternoon rain the windows were thrown back, the wide eaves deflecting the water. Helen watched a tiny lizard run across the screen madly in pursuit of a small spider, and glancing overhead she saw that overnight the webs had gathered and a house spider, large as an inverted teacup, was striding across the beams.

"There's a new cobweb on the *lanai*, Ahulani," she said to the tinkle of approaching glasses without bothering to turn her head.

"Lots of people come tonight?" Ahulani served them iced tea in two tall frosted glasses wrapped in matting.

Helen slouched in a rattan chair. "A good many, Ahulani, it's an easy way for the doctor to repay his social-business obligations — at one blow."

Polly had smiled, shaking her head. "There, you see! *Haoles* like to go to parties but they hate to prepare a feast. . . ."

Helen stiffened. Accused, she tried to see beyond Polly's skillfully composed, smiling features. Finally she nodded apologetically. "Sometimes I think I understand. Something deep inside of me that made me want to dance when I was little, and still wants to dance, but can't — understands you." Helen smiled wryly, embarrassed. She groped for another cigarette and this time carefully shaded the flame from the sunlight.

Jacqueline flung herself against Helen as if seeking embryonic security. "Mother, Mother — I'm not so *really* afraid, but only inside of me — I'm afraid . . . Please . . ." She felt a sudden maddening panic. The fog was everywhere, inside her mind and outside, wetting her hair and swirling around her, hiding everything she tried to see.

Helen was submerged in the cloying pain spreading in her hip. The cold dampness dragged at her sick limbs.

"Mother . . ."

A faint wind stirred, lifting the mists up and away from the waters. Helen stared down the side of the ship where a small black oil-slick was spreading slowly over the sea, opalesque, undulating, a transient burial marker.

It was a shame the victors could not cast a wreath upon the waters. She would have liked that, to express the willy-nilly political currents man followed, had to follow or be killed, and in following was killed. . . . She would have liked to cast a wreath, feeling no rancor in her heart, only an almost mystical wonder at the hazard of living, the terror of dying, and the natural certainty of death.

Someone was laughing and waving a flag produced out of thin air. But better the wreath . . .

Helen was vaguely conscious that Jane had come above deck, leaving Sue huddled in her bunk clutching her baby, and was standing beside her. Both hands, flashing diamonds, were gripping the rail. Her thick shapeless body was hunched over and her eyes flickered with delight. Helen edged away.

"The dirty bastards . . ." Jane whispered finally.

Helen felt the blood rush to her face. No. No. Must we draw and quarter the hanged? Better the wreath and a silent prayer for Kim in death.

Kim, the victim of what? Of race? Of circumstance?

Perhaps the prayer was irony . . . presumptuous. She might have saved him, if she had dared. James had made it an impassable issue, a betrayal of the clan. Helen was white. She was married. She had distinct social obligations to society. Her husband was a doctor. Oh God, the reasons massed themselves into an endless barrier. An uncivilized instinct, such as Ahulani followed when she adopted him into her constantly growing family, had motivated Helen. In the delicacy of her sensitivity, her acquiescence to civilized *Kapu,* Helen had let her maternal instinct harden into a sack of neatly waxed oranges. . . .

≈≈≈≈≈

The last orange fell to the ground, rolled a foot or two, then lay still upon the bilious green moss. The intensity of the two colors vibrated in the noon sun, forming a blurred violet halo around the fruit. Kim did not stoop to pick it up. He feared the pain and dizziness in the awkward unbalance of his crippled body. But it had been good of Mrs. Marin to give it to him.

Slowly Kim climbed from his perch on the bridge railing and began to walk upstream. It was hard to walk, one-armed. Clumsily, he followed the path that he and Jacqueline had made together in their daily forages for water cress. In a moment of memory that left him pained and breathless, he recalled the last time they had walked there. He knew it had not been his place to love Jacqueline, but he couldn't stand being so full of unshared happiness. He ought to have known she would mock him. But for once in his life he had dared to speak like any boy with parents — like someone who really belonged. . . . Ahulani had been everything to him, but she had her own children.

The Ferraras were poor; when their stomachs growled they had always turned on him; and fair and loving though Ahulani was, she had fed them first. It was natural, Kim knew — and it was just as natural that he wanted a share. He had fought to belong.

Here in the upper valley for a moment he had thought he had belonged, just as that night when the *buffa* came and leered, like an avenging devil. But here, with the scarlet cardinal, he knew there were no devils, and he had belonged for a moment with the green grasses and white-hot sun. Today he met the cardinal again and saw, beside the handsome male, his mate.

Soft as the morning mists swept downward from the Pali, this gray lady — orange-billed, hovering shyly, hunting insects within the crannies of volcanic rock . . .

Kim followed the birds as they fluttered, swooping and soaring from stone to tree, up, up the valley to the river's source. Overhead, the first buds were beginning to tint the naked delicacy of the shower-trees with pink and gold. The poinciana was slowly turning scarlet, and the soft spring mists trailed scarves among the trees.

Kim stood very still. His arm ceased to throb

and he lost consciousness of himself. He must not move or breathe! In the long quiet minutes that surged silently one upon the other, as the sun rose higher and higher marking them, Kim heard the trade wind ruffle the palms. A dragonfly zoomed past his head. He heard the machinery of darting bees and the quiet moronic hum of the myriad mosquitoes swarming over the lush carpet of sweet rotting guavas fallen on the ground. He knew that he had but to turn his head to see the source of the stream that bubbled at his feet, the bold upright rock above him. He heard the thread of water falling over it.

Kim felt an unaccountable urge within him, recalling his origin. I was born here! I belong here! The scarlet cardinal flashed by and perched for an instant above Kim's head dipping his wings in the cool water. The gray mate followed. There were always two! Kim felt a sickening gust of agony that came, not from his physical wounds, but deeper within his heart.

That night when he had knocked at the door of the hovel in Pauoa, timidly, despairingly hopeful, Joe Ferrara had met him stony-eyed. He was a big fellow — strong, dark of temper. He had loved Ahulani possessively, passionately. He stood and looked at Kim. And then he turned his back. The young ones, all of them (How Kim loved them! His foster brothers and sisters . . .) seemed somehow to have filled the room, leaving him no corner. Kim had backed away.

Where had he slept since? Kim could not remember. It didn't matter. He crouched by the water staring at the pinched face reflected there. Japanese . . . American . . . Outcast . . . Bastard? His face crinkled, his flat little ivory face with its brooding tiny eyes. Kim longed for Ahulani.

With a tormented sob he began to climb the rock. The way was steep, and the rock pocketed with tiny sharp cups where the once boiling stone had hardened.

The cardinals wheeled past, recklessly plunging down the thread of water. Kim's knees bled, his lungs ached. Hateful resisting stone! Vomit of earth's agony! He was sobbing and the stump of his arm throbbed afresh. Oh, but the stones were brutal! The flashing cardinal again . . . The mists of waterfall wafted across his face . . . Cruel, jagged earth!

Kim no longer knew where or why he climbed. He felt only an impelling hand, warm, as if it might belong to a loved one guiding him. Far below, he heard the cardinal burst into song.

Kim crawled along the face of the cliff and did not feel it cut him. He dragged himself erect, and swaying high above the lily-clogged pool he leaned out and dove among the rocks.

≈≈≈

Standing at the ship's rail, the mists blowing across her face, cooling it, Helen slid her arm across Jane's shoulder.

"It was yellow bastards like that strafed Jack!" Jane murmured. Then she shrugged. Her eyes were dull, her diamonds alone never ceased sparkling. She fumbled all thumbs for her crumpled pack of cigarettes and offered one to Helen.

They bent together for a moment over the match. There was no sun to strike the flame, there was no shadow cast below.

Jacqueline had fallen to her knees, nearly fainting. Her arms were dragging at Helen, who felt the girl's body plunged against hers as if they had always been umbilically joined. Helen bent down, stroking Jacqueline's head.

"Hush, we're all right. . . . Nothing happened to us! See Mrs. Sparrow dancing in a ring with those — those children!"

Even as she helped Jacqueline up the girl tore free, shrieking delightedly.

There was a sudden laugh within the ship. A thousand voices began to chatter.

"The bridge! There — Look, there it is!" Tears and laughter rose in a wave around Helen in her pain.

"The Golden Gate!"

Slowly the span swung overhead. Beyond lay the jumbled city flecked in sunlight. Helen's hand sought Jackie's. The cloying pain in Helen's limbs diminished, became endurable, a purely physical anguish.